# Eleventh Hour Fire!

## (The Burning Heart of Last Day Revival)

Diagnosing and Extinguishing Counterfeit Fires and
Burning with the True Fire of God!

CRAIG YANCY

ISBN 979-8-89428-940-3 (paperback)
ISBN 979-8-89428-941-0 (digital)



Christian Faith Publishing
832 Park Avenue
Meadville, PA 16335
www.christianfaithpublishing.com



Printed in the United States of America

# CONTENTS


Introduction.................................................................v

Chapter 1:  Consuming Fire .........................................1

Chapter 2:  Fear Not!..................................................13

Chapter 3:  The Elements...........................................21

Chapter 4:  Tool or Torment......................................31

Chapter 5:  The Deception .........................................42

Chapter 6:  What's Really Going On? .........................51

Chapter 7:  Extinguishing Toxic Fires.........................57

Chapter 8:  True Fire!................................................70

Chapter 9:  Maintaining the Fire................................83

# INTRODUCTION

WHEN WE SPEAK ABOUT FIRE IN THE context of our Christian walk, it is common for us to think about the fire of the Holy Spirit and sometimes the fire of trials or the refining fire. However, we often fail to recognize the true significance of fire as it relates to the kingdom of God and this life. In Scripture, fire is depicted as having a much more significant role in our lives than just being an analogy. It relates to God's power, manifest presence, and judgment. This was a subject that the Holy Spirit took me deeper into in writing this book, and I pray it helps shed light on the truth of God's Word in your life. This truth, God's truth, always shines light and brings freedom when we sincerely seek to know Him more intimately. Here's what I want to explore with you:

Each of us is a sort of fireplace, metaphorically speaking. Our hearts are the base, or floor, of that fireplace. Whatever fuel is laid down in the base (our hearts) will determine the type of fire that burns within us. Unfortunately, because we live in a fallen world, we all experience the nature of sin both in our own lives and in the lives of those around us. Because of this, the opportunity is given to the enemy to lay down a foundation of toxic materials (sin). When that happens, the sin brings forth a counterfeit flame that can hide for some time but will become increasingly apparent and dangerous as that toxic flame grows. These toxic counterfeit fires can be deceptive, but the damage they cause is real. The good news is that when we experience salvation through faith in Jesus Christ, we have access to the True Fire of God. When God's Word and things pertaining to the kingdom of God are laid at the base of our hearts, then the fire that burns will be pure and genuine and will always bring life. This True Fire only comes through the power of the Holy Spirit.

Here's the bottom line: It is not God's desire or plan for us to live in the bondage, deception, and destruction of sin. He has called us to be His own and to live a full life sold out to His will, kingdom, and divine purpose. It is *not* His will for anyone to perish or be destroyed (2 Peter 3:9) or to live in anything less than an abundant and free life. A life of repentance. A life of victory. A life of freedom. The Lord paid a *very high* price to accomplish this. He gave everything. He gave Himself. That was too high of a price for us to live carelessly with our hearts. We must live with hearts that burn for Him! We must protect that Fire at all costs, and here is the most significant reason for this.

We are truly living in the last days. I believe we live in the last hour, not just the last days—the eleventh hour. We are so close to midnight when Christ will call us home, and so shall we ever be with the Lord. Because we are so close, it's as important as ever that we work diligently to help as many people as possible receive the gospel and lead them to salvation through faith in Jesus. So many people are hurt and feel stuck, hopeless, and afraid. The world is in chaos. But we have the answer, and that answer is found in Jesus. We have been commissioned to work for Him to take the answer to the world in this last hour. The book of Matthew records this statement made by Jesus.

> For the kingdom of heaven is like a landowner who went out early in the morning to hire laborers for his vineyard. Now when he had agreed with the laborers for a denarius a day, he sent them into his vineyard. And he went out about the third hour and saw others standing idle in the marketplace, and said to them, "You also go into the vineyard, and whatever is right I will give you." So they went. Again he went out about the sixth and the ninth hour, and did likewise. And about the eleventh hour he went out and found others standing idle, and said to them, "Why have you been standing here idle all day?"

They said to him, "Because no one hired us."
He said to them, "You also go into the vineyard,
and whatever is right you will receive." (Matthew
20:1–7 NKJV)

Jesus went on to tell us that, in the end, all the laborers were paid the same wage. The ones who went out to work at the eleventh hour were paid the same wage as the ones who went out early in the day. So although the return of Christ is near, it's not too late to work! It is as urgent now as it has ever been that we burn with the Fire of God to labor for His kingdom. We are in the eleventh hour, and the harvest is promised to be great (Luke 10:2)! Now we know that no man knows the day or exact time of His return, but we can follow the signs He gave us to discern the time!

Here's the problem: too many people, including Christians, are living with toxic fires burning in their hearts and minds and are deceived about it. Literally, millions around the world struggle with fear, anxiety, addictions, sickness, distractions, and more. These things keep us from fulfilling our God-given purpose of expanding the kingdom of heaven on earth. The Holy Spirit wants to help us extinguish those toxic fires so the True Fire of God can burn in and through us so that we, by the power of the Holy Spirit, can go and light the world on Fire for Jesus. That we would heal the sick, raise the dead, cast out devils, set captives free, and more. All so that souls would be saved! We need revival Fire! A revival of repentance and fear of the Lord! I believe the Lord is calling you. That's why you have this book in your hands. It's time to find freedom from toxic fires and begin to burn for Jesus!

So here is the challenge for you. As you journey through this book, examine yourself. Challenge yourself as we explore the different fires that can burn in us and allow the Holy Spirit to shine a light on the areas He needs to change. Then let Him make those changes, catch Fire for Jesus, and light the world. Jesus is coming, and we must work for His kingdom to win as many souls as possible.

# CHAPTER 1

# Consuming Fire

FIRE: IT'S INTRIGUING. IT'S POWERFUL. IT'S DANGEROUS. It's useful. It's destructive. It's controllable and yet can be uncontrollable. It refines. It can soften the hardest metals and yet harden soft clay. It's a valuable tool in the hands of a responsible adult, but it can be a tragedy in the hands of a curious child.

But perhaps the most important thing, or at least one of the first things to learn about fire, is that it consumes. That's what it does. That is the primary function of fire. Fire has other effects, like providing warmth and light, but those are secondary to fire's main effect or function. Fire consumes, and the same flame we use to cook and consume impurities from a meal also has the power to become a raging wildfire that consumes everything in its path. Fire can either be used for precision in dealing with issues or it can be let loose to consume everything.

As we progress in this book, we will explore how "fire" can work in our hearts. The ultimate goal for each of us should be to allow the Holy Spirit's Fire to do a precise work in our hearts to refine us and make us vessels through which His fire can spread to others. However, we will discover how bad fires can rage in our lives as a result of sin and also how the Fire of God can be a consuming fire in the final judgment that will consume all sin that is not covered in the Blood of Jesus. So buckle up with me; your path to receiving your already-purchased freedom and victory starts right here, right now!

The Bible tells us that all things were created by the Word of God (John 1:3), so fire didn't just happen; it's part of God's creation. It plays such a massive part in the functions of this world and occurs both naturally, through things like lightning strikes, and purposefully at the hands of people. Fire is such a tremendous force that the word fire occurs over five hundred times in the Bible, and God even uses fire to describe Himself.

In this chapter, we will examine how God relates to the force He created, starting with the following two verses. Moses wrote this first verse as he was recounting instructions that were given to the Israelites before making their way into the promised land, and in the second passage, the writer of Hebrews echoes those instructions to the early church:

> Take heed to yourselves, lest you forget the covenant of the Lord your God which He made with you, and make for yourselves a carved image in the form of anything which the Lord your God has forbidden you. For the Lord your God *is a consuming fire,* a jealous God. (Deuteronomy 4:23–24 NKJV)

> Therefore, since we are receiving a kingdom which cannot be shaken, let us have grace, by which we may serve God acceptably with reverence and godly fear. For our God *is a consuming fire.* (Hebrews 12:28–29 NKJV)

Now let me pause for just a second. If you want to put this book down after reading that God is a consuming fire, don't! Do not let the enemy make you feel afraid of the Lord! That kind of fear that makes you want to run away from God is not from God! I experienced this myself in one of the most challenging spiritual battles of my life. The enemy fought me with so much fear and anxiety that just reading something like God is a consuming fire would set off a whirlwind of mental torment. So I get it, but there is freedom in His truth. Remember, Jesus said the truth will set you free (John 8:32), which is why the enemy tries to strike fear in us. To make us run from God. Don't! Run to Him and His truth: the Word of God!

His love for you is *so great* that He will not let you go! He is so patient and merciful, but also holy. Read Hebrews 12:5–11. If God corrects your thinking about Him or corrects you about sin, it's because He loves you. Any condemnation you feel as you read it is not from God. He does convict us of sin and help us get on the right path, but the Holy Spirit does not bring fear, torment, or condemnation. That's why the enemy will try to drive you away from God's truth. So hang in there. There are a lot of truths from God's Word in the pages that follow, and I pray they will help set you on a path of freedom and to a heart that burns for Jesus.

Okay, back to the subject. The writer of Hebrews shows us we are to serve God with reverence and godly fear. That is to be in awe of God and His great power and glory. The same God who loves you and wants to pour that love on you is also the Creator of the universe. He is King, a righteous judge, and He is as holy as He is loving. His holiness dictates that no sin can be in his presence. The good news is that our heavenly Father made a way for us to be in His presence through the sacrifice of Jesus on the cross.

You don't have to fear the consuming fire when you believe in Christ, because the consuming fire functions for our benefit. We'll talk more about that in a bit. But you cannot get away from the fact that God *is a consuming fire,* and it is imperative that we address this and lay this foundational truth first. There are also great books and teachings about the fear of the Lord and what that means to the believer. We all want to know that our Father loves us, and He does, but ignoring the crucial need to maintain a healthy fear, awe, and respect for Him is dangerous. That's why we must address this first to be properly positioned in Christ to receive the promises discussed in the next chapters.

A significant problem in the contemporary church in America and many places across the earth is the loss of the fear of the Lord. I'll admit that I spent most of my life not understanding, or not discerning, this principle until the Lord so graciously brought me across incredible men and women of God and their books and teachings from scripture that just ripped into my careless way of living as a "Christian." So many believers walk this life thinking we are doing just fine when the truth is we're not fully surrendered. We hold on to control and compromise with sin. We will say we love Jesus but have no genuine, reverent fear of His Majesty and holiness. The Lord described people who draw near to Him with their mouths and honor Him with their lips, but whose hearts are far from Him (Isaiah 29:13; Matthew 15:8). Sadly, this is the condition of many Christians.

A few years ago, I began to feel a stirring inside to draw closer to God. As I started that journey with the Holy Spirit, the refining Fire of God began to bring to the surface in my life so many impurities in my heart, attitude, and thought process, most of which I didn't realize were there. After years of being in the church, I found thought patterns, sins, habits, and ways that seemed right to me (Proverbs 14:12) that God had to reveal and completely dismantle to rebuild my character. It was and still is, at times, a painful process. There came with it a fierce battle with anxiety and fear. But it is in that refining Fire that God brings to the surface and removes those impurities if we cooperate with Him. This is an essential process because most, if not all, of us, at one point or another, have strongholds established in our thought lives that must be torn down. (2 Corinthians 10:4).

Yes, God is a loving Father who desires the best for us. So much so that He paid a very high price for you and me; He gave everything when He sacrificed His Son on the cross! But before we talk about God's love, mercy, kindness, and patience, we *must* remember that He is just as *holy* as He is loving. As much as God desires to be with us, sin *cannot* dwell in His presence (Psalm 5:4–5). Jesus took our sins upon Himself to remedy this. Still, there's a reason why the writer of Hebrews in the New Testament repeated the writings of Moses from Deuteronomy in the Old Testament. It's imperative in the life of every Christian that we maintain a healthy reverence for the holiness of God and not be flippant about sin. We must remember that freedom in Christ is not the freedom to sin but rather freedom from the power of sin over us (Romans 6:6–7). More on this blessed hope later, but stick with me. The purpose of this book is to inspire hope in Christ Jesus for your freedom, but with a solid foundation, so that we can light the world on fire with the supernatural power of God in this last hour!

Let's explore deeper into what Moses was outlining to the people of Israel in this passage in Deuteronomy. Moses gave instructions to the Israelites before entering the promised land, and he recounted to them the experience they had with the Lord when He rescued them from their bondage in Egypt. This was a type of us being rescued from the bondage of sin. The people of Israel had seen and experienced the Lord's power and might. They heard the thunder of His voice from the fire.

> To you, it was shown that you might know that the Lord Himself *is* God; *there is* none other besides Him. Out of heaven, He let you hear His voice, that He might instruct you; on earth, He showed you His great fire, and you heard His words out of the midst of the fire. (Deuteronomy 4:35–36 NKJV)

When the Israelites came out of centuries of bondage in Egypt, the Lord showed Himself mighty to them, and fire was a crucial element in how He manifested Himself. We first see this as the Israelites traveled away from Egypt, and the Lord went before them in a pillar of cloud by day and a pillar of fire by night (Exodus 13:21).

The fire provided light and guided God's people at night as they fled the bondage of Egypt. Exodus 14:20 tells us that when the Israelites came up against the Red Sea and Pharaoh and his army approached from behind, the pillar of cloud in the day and the pillar of fire at night moved behind the Israelites and stood between them and Pharaoh's army, keeping God's people safe. Now we know how the story ends up. The Lord rescued his people, and they crossed the Red Sea on dry land. As Pharaoh and his army tried to chase after the Israelites, the Lord closed the water back up, and the entire Egyptian army drowned to pursue them no more! So God appeared in the pillar of fire as His people's guiding light and protector. This is where most of us want to stop. We think we've got the promise of God's miracles and protection, so we're good.

However, the Lord, who manifested His power through many miraculous signs in Egypt and at the Red Sea, was now about to show up in another significant way. He would display himself in a way that would leave no doubt what it means to have an extraordinary respect, or reverent fear, of the Lord! The Israelites had been led up to Mount Sinai, and God told Moses he wanted to meet with the people. He was about to lay out some instructions. God gave Moses specific instructions that the people were not to go up into the mountain or even touch the border of it. So the people stood at the foot of the mountain, and God showed up!

> And Moses brought the people out of the camp to meet with God, and they stood at the foot of the mountain. Mount Sinai *was* completely in smoke because the Lord descended upon it in fire. Its smoke ascended like the smoke of a furnace, and the whole mountain quaked greatly. (Exodus 19:17–18 NKJV)

Once again, God showed up in fire! As He delivered His instructions on how they should live, the Bible says they heard and saw thunder and lightning, the sound of a loud trumpet, and smoke billowing from the mountain (Exodus 20:18). The Israelites were trembling with fear! I get it. It's hard to imagine seeing and hearing a display of His power like that. Now watch this verse:

> Then they said to Moses, "You speak with us, and we will hear; but let not God speak with us, lest we die." And Moses said to the people, "Do not fear; for God has come to test you, and that His fear may be before you, so that you may not sin." (Exodus 20:19–20 NKJV)

The same God who had just delivered His people from bondage in Egypt with many miraculous signs was preparing the Israelites to move into their destiny and God-given purpose. But first, He showed up in the fire with such a powerful display to achieve this one goal: to test them "that His fear may be before you, so that you may not sin." This is why we start this book with the fear of the Lord and revealing God as a consuming fire. Before God leads you into your destiny, He wants to achieve this same goal in you: "that His fear may be before you so that you do not sin." This is His process of repentance and sanctification, worked by the Holy Spirit to get you to a victorious life in Christ. No, we're not perfect, and yes, we struggle in some areas. *But Jesus did not suffer such a horrific death so that we could embrace the pleasures of sin.*

If you say to yourself, *That's the Old Testament, and God is a loving Father. Jesus died for our sins, and it's the goodness of God that leads to repentance. He's not angry!* Well, you would be incompletely correct. What I mean is this: these things are all correct, but there's more. The Word of God is the authority on this, and yes, the Lord is slow to anger (Nehemiah 9:17; Psalm 145:8), quick to forgive (Psalm 86:5), and Jesus paid the total price for our sins. All who believe and trust in Him receive the gift of salvation (Romans 10:8–10; John 3:16–17; Ephesians 2:8). God loves us. But you need to have the truth, the whole truth, and nothing but the truth if you want to live a free life pleasing to the Father.

Here's the truth: *sin is no longer your nature or your master* (Romans 6:6–7, 11–14; Romans 8:2)! You don't have to settle for the enemy's lies that you can't help or that you'll always give in to sin. The devil will try to keep you in the cycle of falling into sin so he can continue to accuse you (Revelation 12:10) and bombard you with guilt and shame. The enemy does this to keep you out of God's presence and ultimately keep you from fulfilling your purpose. And remember, sin gives the enemy legal access to you that is only remedied by the blood of Christ.

When we maintain a healthy fear and reverence for the Lord as the holy King of kings, we more faithfully follow a life of holiness. Not perfection, but holiness. When you do this, the Holy Spirit works tirelessly to help you overcome any habit or stronghold of sin. And, though we are instructed not to sin (1 John 2:1), He promises that if we do sin, He is *faithful* and *just* to forgive us for those sins and to cleanse us from all unrighteousness (1 John 1:9)! It is a process that is not designed for us to earn God's love and acceptance, but instead to draw us closer to His heart and further from the destruction of sin.

Romans 2:4 tells us that it is the goodness of God that leads us to repentance. But the next verse says that because we are stubborn and refuse to turn from sin, we are storing up terrible punishment on the day of judgment. Yep, that's the New Testament. So yes, God's kindness is intended to turn us from sin, but it is not a license to sin. He does love you with an undying and unfailing love. He is merciful and patient, and He forgives. But living with love for God should lead us to walk with reverent fear and respect for the God who is King and judge. Stay tuned. As we unpack this, we will discover more truth about how to walk this out.

Remember the verses from Deuteronomy and Hebrews that described God as a consuming fire? The question to ask yourself is, How will you face that consuming fire? There are two ways to face the Fire of God. For the believer, the Fire of the Holy Spirit can burn in us daily as it (the Fire) refines us and burns out the junk if we let Him. However, for the unrepentant sinner, it's the consuming fire of God's wrath at His final judgment that sits in wait. The bottom line is that the Fire of God will consume! It will consume all sin *that's not covered in the blood of Jesus.*

> "For behold, the day is coming, burning like an oven, and all the proud, yes, all who do wickedly will be stubble. And the day which is coming shall burn them up," says the Lord of hosts, "That will leave them neither root nor branch. But to you who fear My name, the Sun of Righteousness shall arise with healing in His wings; And you shall go out and grow fat like stall-fed calves." (Malachi 4:1–2 NKJV)

And anyone not found written in the Book of Life was cast into the lake of fire. (Revelation 20:15 NKJV)

But the cowardly, unbelieving, abominable, murderers, sexually immoral, sorcerers, idolaters, and all liars shall have their part in the lake which burns with fire and brimstone, which is the second death. (Revelation 21:8 NKJV)

But He will say, "I tell you I do not know you, where you are from. Depart from Me, all you workers of iniquity." There will be weeping and gnashing of teeth, when you see Abraham and Isaac and Jacob and all the prophets in the kingdom of God, and yourselves thrust out. (Luke 13:27–28 NKJV)

Not everyone who says to Me, "Lord, Lord," shall enter the kingdom of heaven, but he who does the will of My Father in heaven. Many will say to Me in that day, "Lord, Lord, have we not prophesied in Your name, cast out demons in Your name, and done many wonders in Your name?" And then I will declare to them, "I never knew you; depart from Me, you who practice lawlessness!" (Matthew 7:21–23 NKJV)

*Okay, pause.* If you are experiencing anything like what I and countless others have experienced, the enemy tries to wreak havoc on your mind when you read verses like these. The devil will lie to you about God not being good, or that He is good but just not to you, or that you've been too bad to be forgiven; you're rejected, abandoned, and on and on. The enemy's number-one tactic is fear—fear about the future, fear of the past, fear of people, fear of not being good enough, or an *unhealthy* fear of God! The great news is that those are all lies meant to keep you in a cycle of discouragement and defeat that ultimately keep you from doing what the devil himself fears, and that's you fulfilling your God-given purpose for God's kingdom!

The message here is not that you must be perfect. Our perfection is in Christ Jesus. However, we must understand that constantly falling into the cycle of sin is like staying in an abusive relationship. Constant abuse keeps you in a cycle of pain and suffering, both internally and all around you, as sin gives place to the enemy. You know you need to get out of it. You might even be asked by those around you why you keep going back to that abuser (sin). You tell yourself, *This is it; I'm not taking it anymore*, only to find yourself right back in the arms of that same destructive habit that is ready to pounce on you once again. This does not only apply to those outward sins we quickly see, like drug addictions, drunkenness, sexual immorality, pornography, etc., but it also applies to sins of the heart like unforgiveness, bitterness, resentment, hatred, gossip, jealousy, covetousness, deception, and so much more.

The Lord asks you and me to believe in Jesus and truly surrender our lives. This goes much deeper than just saying a prayer to accept Jesus. The Word of God clearly instructs us to repent of our sins. The word *repent* is from the Greek word *metanoeo*, which means to have a change of mind. Your thought process about sin must change. Jesus Himself said we must repent (Matthew 4:17; Luke 13:3), the disciples preached that people should repent (Mark 6:12), and Acts 17:30 says God commands us to repent. There are many more verses, but I believe you get the point.

We must come to a point where we think differently about sin. This is where the reverent fear of the Lord comes in. Understanding that God is entirely holy should drive us away from sin. I covered this above about coming out of an abusive relationship with sin. But this starts by acknowledging that we are all guilty before the Lord. It does not matter how big and bad or how small and insignificant you think your sins have been; violating God's law in any form or measure makes us guilty, and we've all done it. Because of this, we all deserve to be punished.

Sin, in any form or amount, demands eternal separation from God. So you and I are guilty. Acknowledging this is key to walking in repentance. It looks something like this: "Lord, I acknowledge my sins. I am guilty; there's no excuse, and I deserve to be punished. But I thank you that Jesus took that punishment for me by shedding His blood and giving His life on the cross. I also agree that sin, in all forms and measures, is wrong and has no place in my life. I renounce sin and receive your help to walk in victory over it." When we can change our thinking about sin and turn away from it (repent), we start the journey of finding freedom from the sins and habits that weigh us down.

I'll make it clear again: I'm not talking about trying to live good enough or clean enough to earn God's love or forgiveness. Self-righteousness says, *I can be good enough to earn God's pardon, but you can do nothing to be good enough to earn it.* Salvation is a gift paid for by Jesus on the cross. But don't trample on the cross by living in blatant, purposeful, and persistent sin. Stop spitting on the gift. okay, I love you. I know that sounds harsh, but you are worth too much to the Lord not to find your purpose in Christ.

Here's the good news! You can be free from the control of sin! Jesus paid for you and me to have the freedom to live a life consecrated to God. When you put your genuine faith and trust in the blood that Jesus shed for you, confess him as your Savior, and repent of your sins, you are instantly justified before God, and He calls you righteous! The great thing about it is that this is a gift from God.

> For by grace you have been saved through
> faith, and that not of yourselves; it is the gift of
> God. (Ephesians 2:8 NKJV)

Now the consuming Fire of God is no longer the promise of impending judgment in the lake of fire. Instead, it's a refining fire sent to make you who God designed you to be: a child of God who is holy and pleasing to your Father in heaven! You should know that this is a process called *sanctification*. If you spend time daily reading His Word and praying, the Holy Spirit will make you more like Jesus every day. If you make a mistake or fall into a sin, return, acknowledge, and confess it to the Lord immediately, repent, and move forward. You are forgiven and loved by your Father in heaven.

# CHAPTER 2

# Fear Not!

There is only one true Fire. That is the Fire of the Holy Spirit. But, as we progress, I will introduce in more detail the idea that we all experience other fires in our lives that result from sin and mankind's fallen state. These fires are what I call toxic or bad fires, and they are only counterfeits. However, if not dealt with, these toxic counterfeits can have devastating effects. This is why chapter 1 was so important. There's a reason God calls us out of our abusive relationship with sin. Sin can have real consequences, even here on earth. The good news is that God has given us access to His Fire through Jesus, and those tormenting counterfeit fires are no match for the true Fire of God.

Walking in the victory of Christ, however, requires us to begin to fight fire with Fire, but this concept is not the same with God as it is with the world. The worldly definition is to use the same tactics or methods your enemy uses against you, even if those tactics or strategies are considered bad. In other words, you hit or attack me; I hit and attack you back the same way, just as hard or harder, even if it's evil. That's not God's way. The Lord said He will fight our battles (Exodus 14:14; Deuteronomy 1:30). We don't need to use the devil's tactics because Jesus completely disarmed the enemy, and we stand in that victory. The Fire of the Holy Spirit annihilates the counterfeit fires of the enemy. That's what it means to fight fire with Fire in the kingdom of God.

A good analogy for this would be a method sometimes used to help bring forest fires under control or prevent them from starting in the first place. Firefighters will attempt to get ahead of fire by conducting a controlled burn where they purposefully start controlled fires that will burn up the fuel, or dried vegetation, ahead of the raging fire so that when that raging fire reaches the area of the controlled burn, there's no fuel. Everything is already burned up, so the raging fire cannot continue in that direction; instead, it dies out. This is how the Fire of God can work in our lives. We allow the Fire of the Holy Spirit to burn out everything, fueling the toxic fires of the enemy in our lives. This is fighting fire with Fire in the kingdom of God.

It is important to understand, however, that since the devil is no match for God's power, he relies heavily on fear to keep us in sin and defeat. As I mentioned in the first chapter, he often utilizes an unhealthy fear of God to keep us from having peace with God. But here's more of the good news: in the life of the believer, the consuming Fire of God we discussed in chapter 1 takes on a different meaning. Through faith in Christ, those who walk in repentance no longer need to be afraid of God's wrath and righteous judgment against sin on the day of judgment. Being afraid of God and the punishment we all deserve has been taken away when we know the truth! That fear is replaced with a holy, reverent fear and awe for His Majesty, which helps us live out a life that is truly holy. John 8:32 tells us that knowledge of the truth brings freedom. The truth is that I no longer need to be afraid of punishment if I have truly repented and put my faith in Jesus.

> For you did not receive the spirit of bondage again to fear, but you received the Spirit of adoption by whom we cry Abba, Father. (Romans 8:15 NKJV)

Did you catch that? God, who is awesome, majestic, King of the universe, has all power, and has created all things, is your dad! How cool is that? He chose you! You are adopted into the royal family by

His choice! That's how much He loves you. All it takes is for you to make the same choice. Choose Him by placing your genuine faith in Jesus's *huge* sacrifice on the cross.

This is where the consuming Fire plays a new role in our lives. It is the role of sanctification, a process that should work for every true believer. When I place my faith in the blood of Jesus and in His death, burial, and resurrection (Romans 3:22–25, 10:9), I am instantly justified and in right standing with God (Romans 3:24, 28, 4:25, 5:1, 9). Justified means that it is just as if I'd never sinned.

It is important to add a note regarding faith that leads to justification. We must know that when we say we have faith, there should be evidence, and that evidence will be our good works. If we truly believe, it will drive us to produce good fruit through good deeds toward others. To be clear, I'm not talking about doing good works to earn salvation but rather doing good works as a result. So our works or deeds do not make us right or justified before God. It is faith alone. But! Faith is manifested and proven by our works or good deeds (James chapter 2). Good works, good deeds, and giving are what we call faith and love in motion. There are a multitude of examples of this in scripture (James 2:21–25; Hebrews 11:7–31), but the greatest example came from God Himself.

> For God so loved the world that He gave
> His only begotten son, that whoever believes in
> Him should not perish but have everlasting life.
> (John 3:16 NKJV)

God loved us so much that He gave. His love for us drove Him to give. In fact, He loved us so much that He gave His best! He gave everything! The giving and the work of the cross were the proof of Jesus's faith and love for us. He believed that if He endured the cross, He would reap a harvest of souls! So saying we are justified by faith is truth from the gospel, but further truth from the gospel is that faith should show some fruit.

Back to the consuming fire in the life of the believer. Once we are justified, the Holy Spirit begins the process of sanctification (1

Corinthians 6:11). This is the process by which we are separated from sin and transformed to become more like Jesus in the way we think and act. Our hearts are changed. Here is where the fire comes in.

> I indeed baptize you with water unto repentance, but He who is coming after me is mightier than I, whose sandals I am not worthy to carry. He will baptize you with the Holy Spirit and Fire! (Matthew 3:11 NKJV)

This verse is the centerpiece of this book. The Fire of the Holy Spirit is not different from the consuming fire we read about earlier when God showed up in fire on Mount Sinai with the Israelites. It is still the Fire of God. However, for the believer, the consuming Fire of God becomes a sort of tool. We will discuss that aspect more in chapter 4. By the way, the Holy Spirit is not actually a little flame, no more than He is a little dove. The Holy Spirit is the third person of the Godhead. He is the very spirit of the living God! When we talk about the consuming fire or the Fire of the Holy Spirit, we are talking about God's very glory and power!

Now we first come to Jesus with a sinful nature. When we believe in and confess Jesus as Lord and repent of our sins, the old nature is crucified with Christ, and we are resurrected with Him in new life (Galatians 2:20). Water baptism symbolizes this. However, even though we take on the nature of Christ, the sinful nature still tries to hang on, hang around, and hang us up. It fights against the Spirit of God in us (Romans 8:7), and this is where many Christians get caught in a vicious cycle. We discussed this in chapter one. A Christian must not believe the lie that sin is just our nature, and you will always give in. Though it is true that sin will persistently try to get back in, the spirit of God has made you a new creation (2 Corinthians 5:17), and sin is no longer your nature.

We must change our way of thinking. Many of these things are strongholds in our minds and thought patterns that must be torn down and changed (2 Corinthians 10:4–5). This issue goes deeper than just outward sins. This includes heart issues, which are where the real issues are. Most often, the outward sins are just symptoms of what is going on inside our hearts. They can be symptoms of root causes of hurt, pain, abuse, betrayal, rejection, and more.

This is why the Fire of the Holy Spirit is so vital. Jesus said He came to set the captives free (Luke 4:18). Sometimes He does it instantly, but most often, it's a process. This is part of our sanctification. The Holy Spirit brings His Fire to consume and burn out those sins, habits, thought patterns, and weights that set us back and seek to destroy us. It is the refining process. When we sincerely surrender and ask the Holy Spirit to cleanse our hearts, His Fire begins to bring to the surface the issues of the heart. This is just like the process of heating up gold in a fire. As the gold heats up and melts, it will cause impurities to surface. You can then see the impurities and scoop them out, leaving the gold purer. We must know; however, this can be a painful process, but it is worth it to become more like Jesus.

Knowing this, let's go back and look a little deeper into this issue of being afraid as it pertains to the believer. When we make a genuine commitment to Christ, the Holy Spirit dwells in us and immediately begins the good work of perfecting our love for God and others (2 Thessalonians 3:5). We begin the journey of renewing our minds, changing how we think, and thus changing how we live. This all happens as the Fire of God burns in us.

One of the first results should be an increase in our love. Love is an absolute requirement for all who set their hearts to follow Jesus. God is love (1 John 4:8)! Jesus reminded us that the greatest commandment is to love the Lord God with all our heart, mind, soul, and strength, and to love our neighbor as ourselves (Mark 12:30–31). As the love of God is perfected in our hearts, it will drive us to want to please the Father, give ourselves to Him, and long to spend time with Him. We will no longer be afraid of man, circumstances, trials, our past, the future, or even the wrath of God. (Note: this is also a process.) The apostle John put it like this:

> There is no fear in love; but perfect love
> casts out fear because fear involves torment. But

he who fears has not been made perfect in love.
(1 John 4:18 NKJV)

I like the way the New Living Translation lays it out:

Such love has no fear, because perfect love expels all fear. If we are afraid, it is for fear of punishment, and this shows that we have not fully experienced his perfect love. (1 John 4:18 NLT)

As we grow in our love for God and others and in our understanding of God's love for us, the love of God becomes perfected in us, and the automatic result is the expulsion of fear. However, there is a very important key in this verse: "If we are afraid, it is for fear of punishment." When we fear God's punishment, that fear is generally caused by one of two things. The first would be that you have already repented of your sins and are daily walking for the Lord. You might periodically make a mistake or mess up, but you repent and are being sanctified daily. However, you have a lack of knowledge or understanding of the character of God as your loving Father and a lack of understanding of how powerful the blood of Jesus is! When we view God as anything other than who He truly is, we become open to the lies of the enemy and even our own twisted views of what a father is. This is an awful place to be because it breeds torment and fear and erodes our confidence in the Father's faithful love, mercy, and forgiveness through Jesus.

I experienced this firsthand in my own life. As the refining process began, it brought out so many things in my heart that I didn't realize were there. Some things I did know, but even those were highlighted to shed light on the destructive thought patterns working against God's plan for my life. It's painful and exposes how much we need the Holy Spirit burning in our hearts.

One of the biggest things I experienced was a constant fear that the Lord had rejected me, the Holy Spirit had abandoned me, it was too late, God was angry, and so many more lies about the character of

God. I wasn't walking in fear and awe of God, but rather, I was afraid of God. This fear was, I believe, a combination of a demonic attack and a battle with my own thoughts, strongholds, and preconceived ideas of who God is as a father. Most of it was irrational fear, and many of those ideas were formed by religion and issues created out of my experiences. But they were also a result of my own stupidity. It is vital that we are always open and honest with ourselves and especially with God. He knows the deepest secrets of our hearts, so be honest with Him, make no excuses, don't try to justify anything, and have conversations of confession and repentance with the Lord.

I recall the Lord speaking to me one evening when praying about how David related to God in the book of Psalms, and I compared that to how I was feeling. I thought of the difference between David's confidence in God and my struggles. I believe I heard the Lord tell me the difference was that David knew God's character as Father and I didn't. I did not sense it as a statement of rejection but rather a call to get to know Him as a father. I had to learn who God is as a Father, and I knew I had to get to know God's character. It was an invitation.

After reading a book by a well-known minister, I took up his challenge to read Psalm chapter 23 every day for forty days. I asked Jesus what He wanted to show me as I read. It was powerful, as He revealed so much about God's character as it related to me.

I also began a journey through the Psalms to see what all the Psalmists wrote about God. King David asked God for many things, but when it came to attributing titles or attributes to God or His character, David consistently described God's mercy, faithfulness, power, unfailing love, and so much more. And yes, David even described the fear of the Lord and God's disdain for sin and wickedness.

However, even in this process, fears fight hard to hold on, but it takes persistence. It is a fight! You must fight; don't give up. Our minds can only be renewed and the enemy's voice silenced through persistent prayer, fasting, study of the scriptures, and even counseling or help from trusted people of God. These principles create an environment welcoming to the Holy Spirit, and He always brings Fire!

Going back to 1 John 4:18, the second reason one would fear God's punishment is that you haven't truly repented or are still persistent in sin. You haven't received the revelation from scripture that sin is no longer your nature when you truly belong to Christ. Continued sin keeps a fear of punishment in our lives. If you live in sin with no fear of punishment, something's wrong. We must understand that we are made in the likeness and image of God. We are to come out of sin. Yes, it is a process, but that process will never start if we don't fully embrace the fact that God is holy, and when we came to Jesus, sin lost its dominion over us and has no place in our lives. This is the first step in repentance. As we learn the character of God as Father, understand the fear and awe of God, and surrender to the Holy Spirit's work, the Fire of God will burn in us in the process of refining. His Fire will also give us confidence in our relationship with God. Then our declaration becomes this:

> For God has not given us a spirit of fear but of power and love and a sound mind. (2 Timothy 1:7 NKJV)

So we don't have to be afraid of God as His children. We can be confident in the complete work of Jesus on the cross, His redemptive power, and the absolute love God has for us as our Father. His Fire is for our benefit. His Fire will refine us and spread to others. His Fire will destroy the toxic fires burning in us. But again, it is a process that takes time, so if you mess up during the process, don't give up. Confess it to Him, repent again, and keep going. You will see victory with the right mindset and foundation. Let's go deeper into the fire and prepare to burn within for Jesus as your life transforms into His likeness!

# CHAPTER 3

# The Elements

I WANT TO DIG DEEPER INTO THE idea of fire burning in our hearts or our fireplace. Chapters 1 and 2 laid a basic foundation for the importance of understanding the role the Fire of God plays in our lives. We covered a lot, but there is so much more to the Fire of God. I recommend you keep reading and dig deeper into Scripture. But the idea was for us to see the importance of allowing God's Fire to burn in us. As we progress, we will also look at the different kinds of fires that try to mimic the Fire of God. These are fires that are destructive and harmful by nature. More on that in the next chapter, but let's examine some key points about fire since that's the theme God has given us in this book.

As I began studying fire and fireplaces further, I found something interesting. I found that the floor or base of a fireplace is called a *hearth*. I relate this to the topic in this book because the fireplace, or the place where the fire burns or should burn in our lives, is our heart. Proverbs 4:23 (NKJV) says, "Keep your heart with all diligence, for out of it spring the issues of life." Our heart is the floor or seat of the issues burning in us.

The fact that the fireplace floor is called a *hearth* is, I believe, no coincidence. The seat of our hearts must be kept clean and protected. This is nonnegotiable because we have a purpose and a divine destiny, and fulfilling that purpose is contingent upon the condition of our hearts. That's why it's important to ask yourself: What kind of fire is burning there? As you ponder that question, consider this:

Fire needs three basic elements: heat, fuel, and oxygen. Without any one of these, the fire goes out. We will explore each of these as they relate to our lives.

*Heat*

There are two basic sources of "heat" that spark the fires that burn in our lives. The first and most important source is the Spirit of God. I'll explain, but stay with me for a moment as I lay the foundation.

Natural light, even from the sun, as designed and created by God, is the direct result of intense energy and heat. There's a lot of science behind the different ways that process works in the sun, fire, and other light sources. I won't pretend I know all about it. I'm definitely not a scientist. However, I did find in my limited research that intense energy and heat produce light. With that in mind, let's look at the creation story in Genesis.

> In the beginning God created the heavens and the earth. The earth was without form, and void; and darkness was on the face of the deep. And the Spirit of God was hovering over the face of the waters. Then God said, "Let there be light" and there was light. And God saw the light, that it was good; and God divided the light from darkness. God called the light day and the darkness he called night. So, the evening and the morning were the first day. (Genesis 1:1–5 NKJV)

Okay, now follow me. First, everything on earth was covered in darkness. There was no light. The Holy Spirit was hovering over the face of the deep. The earth was covered in water and darkness. God the Father spoke, and that spoken Word from God was, of course, a manifestation of Jesus. He is the Word! God said, Let there be light, and *bam*! The darkness was dispelled by the light.

So question: Where did the light come from? I mean, yes, we know God created it, but what was causing it? What did God create that illuminated everything? Was it the sun? No, the sun, moon, and stars were not created until day four of creation (Genesis 1:14–19).

Here's what I submit, which I believe scripture bears out. The light that burst forth on day one was not produced by the sun's heat because the sun wasn't created until day four. The light was produced from the Fire of God Himself! Several times in scripture, the Lord's presence was manifested as Fire and Light. Not that God is simply a literal fire or light. The Bible says that God is a spirit, and those who worship Him must worship Him in spirit and in truth (John 4:24). But there is so much power and glory in who He is that He is absolutely beaming with Fire and Light!

If you're scratching your head at this idea, look at what the Bible says about it. God is a consuming Fire (Hebrews 12:29). He showed up in Fire on Mount Sinai to speak to the Israelites (Exodus 19:17–18). Moses encountered God speaking to him in a burning bush (Exodus 3:2). A chariot of fire separated Elijah and Elisha before Elijah was taken to heaven in a whirlwind. In fact, even the horses pulling the chariot appeared as fire (2 Kings 2:11). The apostle Paul encountered Jesus and said there was a light that shined brighter than the noonday sun (Acts 26:13). The eyes of Jesus were described by the apostle John as being like a flame of fire (Revelation 1:14). Jesus Himself said He is the Light of the world (John 8:12). There are the three Hebrew boys saved in the fiery furnace (Daniel chapter 3), the fire from God that consumed the water-drenched sacrifice, and the altar during Elijah's confrontation with the prophets of Baal (1 Kings chapter 18). There's more, but I hope we're getting it.

When it comes time to dispel darkness, God is not looking for a box of matches or a flashlight. All the Holy Spirit needs is for the Word of God to be spoken, and *bam*! The Fire of the Holy Spirit burns, and light comes! That's why the Holy Spirit was hovering over the face of the deep. He brought the heat and was just waiting for the

Word to spark the Fire so He could burn brightly, revealing God's glory. If you're thinking that sounds a little out there, look at this:

> The city had no need of the sun or of the moon to shine in it, for the glory of God illuminated it. The Lamb is its light. (Revelation 21:23 NKJV)

This is a description of heaven. There is no sun there. God illuminates it. The Lamb is its Light. So it wasn't the sun when everything lit up on earth on day one of creation. I believe it was the Fire and glory of God Himself. He created the earth as it is in heaven (Matthew 6:10), and if the glory of God illuminates heaven, then I believe the glory, power, and Fire of God illuminated the earth on day one of creation.

This is the source of heat needed for the believer to burn with the Fire of God. The resurrection power of the Holy Spirit is that heat source. I in no way want to be irreverent to the Holy Spirit, but I kind of see it like this. His power is a flame that is always burning, much like a pilot light that stays lit, waiting for someone to turn the gas fully on. That pilot light, so to speak, has behind it the full storage of natural gas. It's just controlled. But open the lines, and the fire will burn!

How do we turn on the gas? We must make a conscious decision to receive the heat source. We must receive and develop a relationship with the Holy Spirit. We can have communion and fellowship with Him (2 Corinthians 13:14). Once we decide to follow Jesus, it is imperative that we partner with the Holy Spirit as our source of heat if we ever hope to burn for Jesus. There are other elements of fuel and oxygen needed for a fire, but we will get to that.

Before proceeding, let me say again that I do not want to be irreverent to the Father, the Son, or the Holy Spirit. I'm just using "heat," "fuel," and "oxygen" as an analogy. We must never forget that the Holy Spirit is the third person of the Godhead—the very Spirit of God!

Continuing with the element of heat, the second source of heat that can spark a fire in our lives is in our souls. The soul is our mind, the seat of our emotions, our will, and the place where we make our choices. The soul is the battleground where everything "heats up." (2 Corinthians 10:3–5; Romans 7:23). The heat of the battle and friction are in the battles of the mind, causing heat that can spark unwanted flames. Whatever fuel gets placed or dumped here will begin to burn because our thought patterns will ignite it.

The friction from the battles in our minds can be a source of heat that causes unwanted fires to burn in us. My pastor calls it "stinkin thinkin." That's why we must grasp this truth.

> For though we walk in the flesh, we do not war according to the flesh. For the weapons of our warfare are not carnal but mighty in God for pulling down strongholds, casting down arguments and every high thing that exalts itself against the knowledge of God, bringing every thought into captivity to the obedience of Christ. (2 Corinthians 10:3–5 NKJV)

It is so important that we get our thoughts in line with God's Word and pull down the thought patterns that are contrary to God. As we study His Word and think about those things that are true, noble, just, pure, lovely, and of a good report (Philippians 4:8), we create a welcoming mindset for the Holy Spirit. He then brings His Fire and begins to burn in us. This is much better than allowing thought patterns that spark destructive fires. Chapter 4 will deal a bit more with how those fires work.

*Fuel*

Every fire needs something to consume—something that keeps it going. This is the fuel. In a nice, cozy fireplace, it's clean-burning wood. In the life of the true Christian, that clean burning wood, or fuel for the Fire of God burning in our hearts, is the Word of God and the things pertaining to His kingdom. In a toxic fire, it might be trash or toxic materials. These toxic materials are sin and the things of this world. Fire will consume, but it's the fuel that determines the type and effects of the fire.

Remember this from the introduction: each one of us is a sort of fireplace? Whatever fuel is laid down in the fireplace bed (our hearts and minds) will determine the type of fire that burns within us. When a genuine bed of God's truth is laid at the surface of our hearts, then the fire that burns in us will be pure and profitable for light, warmth, and a source of comfort, and it can burn off any trash or sin that is set on top of it or that tries to settle into our hearts.

However, when that God-given Fire is either allowed to burn out or is not established in the first place, then room and opportunity are afforded to the enemy to lay down a foundation of toxic materials (sin) that were not meant to burn in us. If that sin is allowed to become the bed of fuel for the fire, it brings forth a flame that will try to imitate the Fire of God, but the results and effects are much different and become increasingly obvious and dangerous as the toxic flame grows.

So there is clean fuel, clean wood, which is the Word of God, love, righteousness, justice, peace, mercy, and all the principles of the kingdom. Then there is dirty or toxic fuel, which is everything else related to sin and this world, like abuse, hatred, sexual immorality, divisions, and so much more. What we allow, what we pursue and seek after, and what is perpetrated against us are all ways fuel gets added to our hearts and minds—our fireplaces.

As a side note, it is important to remember that it's not just us who stack wood or add fuel for the fires in our lives. The people around us are wood stackers as well. It's important that we guard our hearts and minds and not give anyone and everyone permission or access to throw toxic material into our "fireplace" through their influences.

Another very significant aspect of this is that we don't always have control over the wood stacking process. This is especially true for children and the more vulnerable. There is so much absolute tragedy perpetrated against people through abuse, neglect, manipulation, control, and other ungodly acts. This junk often creates very toxic fires in the lives of victims that can take years to clean out. So if you're someone who has influence on others at any level, make sure you read chapter 7 carefully.

*Oxygen*

The final element needed for fire to exist is oxygen. Without oxygen, a fire cannot continue to burn. Have you ever tried starting a campfire with just a little kindling, a striker, or a match? I'm not talking about dousing the pile with gas and throwing a match on it. I'm talking about starting that little flame, hoping it catches and grows. What do you do when you see a little flame or embers? You breathe on it! You fan the flames! Why? Because the oxygen causes the fire to grow.

We already know where the heat and fuel come from. I submit to you that the element of oxygen is directly related to what we are breathing into the fires in our lives in the form of our words. Good or bad, our breath carries a level of oxygen, as does God's breath.

I'm not a doctor, but my- limited knowledge and research have found that we need oxygen to survive. We breathe in a certain percentage of oxygen, and our lungs transfer it to our blood, which then carries the oxygen to the cells of our body, which need it to sustain life. But then there is a gas exchange, and when we exhale or breathe out, there is a lower level of oxygen and a higher level of carbon dioxide. God designed us that way. Look at this passage about the creation of man:

> And the Lord God formed man of the dust
> of the ground and breathed into his nostrils the
> breath of life; and man became a living being.
> (Genesis 2:7 NKJV)

As God breathes and speaks, life always comes forth. His breath was and still is the "oxygen" man needed to sustain life. When we speak or breathe out, the oxygen levels are lower, but the carbon dioxide, or "waste gas," levels are higher. What I'm saying is this: if you want to breathe higher levels of oxygen (life) onto the Fire of God in your life to fan the flames of God, then you must breathe the breath, or Word, of God. The only thing with enough oxygen to fan the flames of God's Fire is His Word.

As an analogy, the Word of God is the oxygen that brings and sustains spiritual life. That's why in Genesis chapter 1, when God said, Let there be light, the Word from the heart of God was the fuel and the spoken or breathed Word was the oxygen. The Holy Spirit was the heat source (power), and the combination was combustible, resulting in God's Fire radiating light to dispel the darkness.

Again, heat, fuel, and oxygen are just analogies, but the principle is this: when we stack the Word of God in our hearts and minds as our fuel, the Holy Spirit is waiting for us to breathe and speak that Word, and He then is the power that backs it up—Fire! The entire earth was created that way. God the Father declared the Word (Jesus), and the Holy Spirit worked!

Just to provide a little more from scripture about the role of oxygen, the spoken Word of God, in creation, look at Hebrews 11:3. It tells us that the Word of God framed the world. John 1:1–3 says that the Word was in the beginning, the Word was with God and was God, and everything was created by the Word. Verse 14 of that same chapter tells us the Word became flesh. That's Jesus! Here's another powerful verse:

> It is the Spirit who gives life; The flesh prof-
> its nothing. The words that I speak to you are
> spirit, and they are life. (John 6:63 NKJV)

There are a few powerful principles in that verse. I want to highlight two of them. The first, we already covered—the words of Jesus bring life. The second, though, is that human effort accomplishes nothing—not for the kingdom of heaven or for fanning the Fire of God. Yes, we are required to partner with God, but efforts on our own are futile.

On the flip side of that, when we lend our tongue to speaking negative, cursing, filthy communication, and anything contrary to God's Word, we actually add an additional spark to starting ungodly fires in our lives.

> In the same way, the tongue is a small thing
> that makes grand speeches. But a tiny spark can
> set a great forest on fire. And among all the parts
> of the body, the tongue is a flame of fire. It is
> a whole world of wickedness, corrupting your
> entire body. It can set your whole life on fire, for
> it is set on fire by hell itself. (James 3:5–6 NLT)

Wow! So in Genesis, we see how the spoken Word of God has the power to spark a fire that lights the whole world! But in James, we see how the spoken words that are contrary to God can spark a fire that sets your whole life on fire by hell itself. So if you're seeing a bunch of ungodly fires burning in your life, make sure you are repentant of your sins, but also check your speech! What is coming out of your mouth about your own life or the lives of others?

When we breathe or speak contrary to God's Word, we are sparking and fanning the wrong flames and providing oxygen to the wrong fires. Yes, we breathe out carbon dioxide, but even in the natural world, we still breathe out some oxygen at lower levels. So stop breathing (speaking) low-level oxygen (negativity) onto the worldly fires; stop complaining; and start breathing the pure oxygen of God, His Word, and fan the flames of the Fire of God in your life!

A final thought on the elements needed for fire to survive. When a fire is to be extinguished, it is necessary to take out at least one of the three elements. Firefighters either remove the heat, usually by dousing the fire with water or some other agent, or remove the fuel source by controlled burns or some other method of clearing out the fuel. The third element of oxygen must be redirected and used to feed the good fires in controlled burns.

The next chapter will explore more of what these fires look like. As you proceed, keep these principles of the elements in mind. I pray it helps us discern some of the things burning in our lives and the provisions God has already made through Jesus to extinguish the bad fires and then cause the Fire of God to burn in us!

# Tool or Torment

WE'VE COVERED A LOT ABOUT GOD AS a consuming Fire and how the Holy Spirit works in the life of the believer as a Fire that burns for Jesus. A Fire that burns away sin, fear, and the things of this world. A Fire that burns with power and can burn within us as love for God the Father and others. We've discussed the elements that make a fire burn, whether it's a good fire or a bad fire. I want to explore a little further the two basic functions of the fires that burn in our hearts and minds. They either function as a tool or as torment. As we explore these, examine yourself to see. Are the fires burning in my life burning as a tool, or are they bringing torment? Let's lay out the differences between the two.

*Tool*

A good, clean, and well-maintained fire has always been a useful tool for man. It is used as a torch to light the way; it sterilizes, refines, melts, gives warmth, and more. All these benefits we enjoy from fire in nature reflect how the Fire of God works as a tool in the spiritual sense. I want to revisit the following verse that we explored in chapter 2:

> I indeed baptize you with water unto repentance, but He who is coming after me is mightier than I, whose sandals I am not worthy to carry.

He will baptize you with the Holy Spirit and Fire!
(Matthew 3:11 NKJV)

The only true, clean fire that can burn in the life of a believer is the Fire of God's spirit. It's a Fire that will always work as a tool in the life of a believer. In chapter 2, we talked about how this Fire functions to burn out and consume sin. This is the refining process. It is the process of sanctification. We touched on this a bit in previous chapters, but there are some practical truths that should be applied for this process to begin in our lives. Let's start with what Jesus had to say about the importance of the Holy Spirit:

> And I will pray the Father, and He will give you another Helper, that He may abide with you forever—the Spirit of truth, whom the world cannot receive, because it neither sees Him nor knows Him; but you know Him, for He dwells with you and will be in you. (John 14:16, 17 NKJV)

> But the Helper, the Holy Spirit, whom the Father will send in My name, He will teach you all things, and bring to your remembrance all things that I said to you. (John 14:26 NKJV)

> But I will send you the Advocate—the Spirit of truth. He will come to you from the Father and will testify all about me. (John 15:26 NLT)

> But you shall receive power when the Holy Spirit has come upon you; and you shall be witnesses to Me in Jerusalem, and in all Judea and Samaria, and to the end of the earth. (Acts 1:8 NKJV)

Jesus made it clear to His disciples and to us that once He ascended to heaven and was taken from this earth, the Holy Spirit would come and be inside each of us who belong to the Lord Jesus Christ. There are some definite works (tools) that the Holy Spirit brings into the life of the believer. I'll highlight a few ways the Fire of the Holy Spirit works as a tool in our lives, but the list is endless and beyond our grasp. Again, I'm not reducing the Holy Spirit to a tool. I'm using an analogy for the Fire that He brings to work in our lives. We're talking about the same Spirit who raised Christ from the dead (Romans 8:11). Do not forget that He is the third person of the Godhead and is to be honored and respected. If you do not have the Spirit of God dwelling in you, then you don't get the tools (fire) that come with Him.

Jesus called the Holy Spirit the helper. One translation says He is our advocate. There are so many teachings on the Holy Spirit by men and women of God who have so wonderfully explained from Scripture who He is and His work on earth. I highly suggest a deeper dive into getting to know Him and His work in your life. But the purpose of this book is to bring to light the different fires that burn in our lives and to bring some basic truths that will hopefully set you on a path of burning wholeheartedly for Jesus so you can fulfill your destiny in Him! This will require allowing the Holy Spirit to extinguish the bad fires and ignite the Fire of God.

So again, Jesus called the Holy Spirit our helper. This is from the Greek word *parakletos,* which means someone called to one's side, pleading another's case, being an advocate, or being an intercessor. Basically, He comes alongside us and is in us to accomplish what Jesus said in the verses quoted above. He brings the words of Jesus to our remembrance. He brings understanding, helps us when we don't even know we need help, and makes intercession for us when we don't know what to pray for (Romans 8:26). When the Fire of the Holy Spirit is burning within our hearts, it causes the scriptures to illuminate our path (Psalm 119:105).

The other significant tool we receive when the Fire of the Holy Spirit comes upon us is the power to be a witness (Acts 1:8)—a witness of His power! It is the power to see the kingdom of heaven manifested here on earth (Matthew 6:10).

> The Spirit of the Lord *is* upon Me, because
> He has anointed Me to preach the gospel to *the*
> poor; He has sent Me to heal the brokenhearted,
> to proclaim liberty to *the* captives and recovery of
> sight to *the* blind, *to* set at liberty those who are
> oppressed. (Luke 4:18 NKJV)

This was Jesus quoting the Old Testament prophecy from Isaiah 61:1 about Himself. But remember that Jesus told his disciples that the works He was doing they, and all who believe in Him, would do also, and even greater works (John 14:12).

Going back to the first two chapters of this book, we understand that the work of the Holy Spirit to burn out sin and make us more like Jesus every day is for this one cause, the cause of Christ, to proclaim the gospel. Proclaim it in the way we live, the way we love, and the way we speak! It was the Fire of God burning in the apostle Paul that gave him the ability to say this:

> And my speech and my preaching *were* not
> with persuasive words of human wisdom, but
> in demonstration of the Spirit and of power. (1
> Corinthians 2:4 NKJV)

The Fire, the work of the Holy Spirit, is what was given to us through the sacrifice of Jesus, so we, too, can preach the gospel to the poor, heal the brokenhearted, proclaim liberty to the captives, bring recovery of sight to the blind, and set at liberty those who are oppressed! To demonstrate the culture of heaven! And guess what? That promise of healing, liberty, and recovery is for you too! When you bring together the correct heat, fuel, and oxygen into your life, the Fire of God will ignite and will have the right tool for what ails you, and you shall be free! When you get to know the truth of God's Word, the truth will set you free! (John 8:32)

To be practical, the way we do this is quite simple. But the actual heavy lifting is not always so simple. It's like lifting weights or working out. The steps are so simple that they can usually be explained in a few pictures or sentences. But lifting the weights is where the real work comes in. We believe and accept Jesus, are baptized in water, repent of our sins, and invite the Holy Spirit to come alongside us and be our helper! As we study the Word and develop an active life of prayer and worship, fasting, and fellowship with other believers, the Fire of God grows in us, our hearts are transformed, and we become empowered to live free and to demonstrate that power to others. But the heavy lifting is more than just doing the things I just listed. The bigger the bad fires are in our lives, the greater the torment brought by those fires, and that's where the real heavy lifting comes in because it will require you to be disciplined and intentional.

*Torment*

I don't even know where to start. There are so many tormenting fires burning in the lives of people that I don't think we could list them all. I'll address some more common ones we must fight to extinguish. But let's first address what we mean by tormenting or bad fire. Remember that the devil tries to imitate God (2 Corinthians 11:14). Chapter 5 deals more in-depth with this deception, but just like God wants to burn bright in us, the devil wants to imitate God by burning his tormenting fires in our lives to keep us from fulfilling our destiny for the kingdom of God.

Thanks be to God, no matter how many tormenting fires there are or how big and bad they seem, they cannot even begin to compare to the power and victory found in Jesus! Access to this power and victory lies within our trust and surrender to Jesus. Understanding the following principles will help us recognize our areas of need to surrender them to the Holy Spirit.

Any fires that burn within us with greater influence, control, and desire than the Holy Spirit's influence, control, and desires are bad fires. The problem with many of these types of fires is that they can sometimes be hard to recognize. When the subtle fires of idolatry, pride, hypocrisy, self-righteousness, religion, legalism, and others are burning in us, they can be hard to recognize because the flames so closely try to imitate the true Fire of God. In Luke 11:35, Jesus said to be careful that what you think is light in your eye is not actually darkness. That's why these toxic fires are so dangerous because they give just enough light to make you think everything is illuminated, but it's dim enough to hide the darkness that sits deep inside. So there's just enough truth and religion to make us feel like we're okay.

If you are or have been battled in any way like I was, then you know that the enemy will try to strike you with an unhealthy fear of the above statement I made. You'll wonder excessively if you are deceived, thinking you have light but are actually full of darkness, and maybe this equates to you being rejected or condemned. I hate the devil and his tactics. Don't let it become an excessive and tormenting fear. However, I do think we absolutely should examine ourselves in these areas (2 Corinthians 13:5). There is an answer to this darkness, and it lies in our genuine surrender to the work of the Holy Spirit. It lies in our ability to be open and honest with God; truly examine ourselves against the Word of God; get rid of pride, hypocrisy, and self-righteousness; and be willing to repent of the things He shows us.

There are other bad fires that are not so subtle, and they burn hot; they manifest in crazy ways, can be very toxic, and often bring varying levels of torment to not just us but also to those around us. I won't be able to list them all, but I'll try to cover some of the more recognizable ones. As you read this, examine yourself and see what is burning in your life with greater influence, control, and desire than that of the Holy Spirit. What keeps you from seeing your character become more like the character of Christ?

One of the biggest categories of tormenting fires is, of course, sexual immorality. This encompasses everything dealing with sex, including adultery, fornication, pornography, and so much more. Sexual immorality has no place in the life of the believer (Acts 15:20; 1 Corinthians 6:18; 1 Thessalonians 4:3; 2 Timothy 2:22).

Have you ever wondered why sexual immorality is such a huge part of the devil's bag of temptations and why sex gets so twisted by sin? I believe it's because sex, within the confines of the marriage covenant relationship between a husband and a wife, reflects the intimate covenant relationship we are to have with God the Father in the spirit. I'm not saying our relationship with God is the same as sex in a marriage. I'm saying that the union enjoyed between husband and wife in a marriage covenant through sex is representative of the close spiritual intimacy the Father desires to have with each of us through communion and fellowship with the Holy Spirit. The devil works to twist and destroy that union.

Sex within the confines of marriage between a man and a woman was also designed by God for us to be fruitful and multiply (Genesis 1:28). This reflects how God's kingdom works. He is the God of multiplication. He creates life and growth. Remember, Jesus said to pray "on earth as it is in heaven." It's no wonder satan attacks the very thing that is meant to bring intimate relationships in marriage, new life, and multiplication on earth. The devil's plan is to steal, kill, and destroy (John 10:10). What better way to accomplish that than to attack the thing that is designed to bring union, fruit, and multiplication?

Every time a person falls into any form of sexual immorality, they stack more and more trash in their fireplace (heart), and they feed that toxic fire. Every pornographic image viewed, every ungodly sexual act of whatever sort it might be, every lustful thought allowed to linger and be pondered, and every filthy communication from our mouth of a perverted sexual nature are all things that have a profound impact on building a raging fire of lust and immorality that, if not dealt with through true repentance, will eventually lead to a wildfire of destruction. You also open yourself to demonic spirits stepping in and taking control. If you've been on this path or maybe already experienced the out-of-control fire of torment from this, there is always hope in Jesus. Make sure you pay attention to chapter 6. The Holy Spirit will deliver all who call on the name of the Lord (Joel 2:32; Romans 10:13).

Another group of fires of torment is rage and anger. These, along with their cousins—frustration, irritability, agitation, and others—are most often fires that have at their root or base other more significant issues. A person is often angry, irritable, frustrated, etc., because of emotional torment stemming from past or current trauma and abuses perpetrated against them or stemming from the torment of guilt, shame, and condemnation constantly eating at their conscience because of past and/or current failures. An important key that is often hidden in this is the need for true and full forgiveness. Holding unforgiveness, resentment, and bitterness is a trap from the enemy that will leave a door open for the devil. Remember, Jesus said if we don't forgive others for their sins, neither will our heavenly Father forgive us (Matthew 6:15). *Note*: This also includes forgiving ourselves!

Forgiveness is so much more than just saying the words "I forgive." Although that is the start. You must confess it. But Jesus said to forgive from the heart (Matthew 18:35). This is often a process that begins with recognizing your need to forgive. There are some good teachings out there on the traps we fall into when we hold unforgiveness, bitterness, and resentment against others or ourselves. Please get those teachings, but if you don't, at least hear this. When you think about what God has forgiven you for and what you want His attitude to be toward you, it will help you try to have the same heart of mercy and forgiveness toward others. In other words, if you knew God would only forgive you to the extent and with the same attitude as you forgive others, you would make every effort to make sure your forgiveness of others and of yourself was top-notch and complete.

If you are saying to yourself that you are good and have forgiven everyone, including yourself, I want you to examine yourself to test if that's true. Do you still battle guilt, shame, or condemnation about your own failures? Have you truly forgiven yourself? When you think about or see the people who hurt or offended you, do ugly feelings immediately surface, like feelings of revenge or anger that they haven't paid for what they did? Things like this should indicate that maybe we still have some work to do. It is a process. Eventually, you can say that the person is released; they owe me nothing, as if they never hurt me in the first place. Now you may still have to set boundaries to stay safe and not give offenders access to hurt you again, but in your heart, you can be free from the power of offense, unforgiveness, bitterness, resentment, and more.

The last group I'll cover—but there are so many more—are the fires of fear, anxiety, and worry. We covered a few scriptures in chapter 2 about fear. Fear has torment (1 John 4:18). There is foreboding fear—fear of something bad coming, fear of the past, fear of rejection, and so on. Fear and anxiety usually work hand in hand as anxious thoughts race through our minds. Most often, fear is irrational, but I can tell you from experience that it doesn't seem irrational when you're going through it. Every fearful and anxious thought seems to make perfect sense. The enemy sometimes creates circumstances, brings dreams, and other stuff to puff up lies and increase fear. He'll even quote scriptures to you! (Matthew 4:6). I heard a pastor say, maybe not in exact words, that fear will always attract whatever information it needs to legitimize its existence.

Of course, there is a natural and good fear that should keep us from things that are harmful. There is also the wonderful fear of God, which helps us walk in awe and respect for who He is. But we are talking about irrational and tormenting fears that are not from God, and that drives us away from God. The goal of the enemy with these fears is to keep us from fulfilling our destiny in Christ and ultimately destroy us. But remember, Jesus defeated satan and the kingdom of darkness, and we no longer have to be slaves to fear!

We can go on about other fires like rejection, addictions, complacency, gluttony, overindulgence, and so many more. But the principles we are covering are the same for all of them. The Fire of God can burn in our lives, but there are these fires of torment that most, if not all, people experience to some degree in their lives. We must extinguish these fires of torment with the truth of God's Word and begin to burn with the true Fire of God. This way, we can impact this world for Jesus so that His kingdom will manifest on earth as it is in heaven.

Before ending this chapter, I want to briefly answer the question of what the heat, fuel, and oxygen for these bad fires look like and where they come from. The heat source, again, is in our patterns of thought. Our carnal, or natural way of thinking, already wants to flow with our sinful nature. We see this described clearly in the book of Romans. All that our minds need is to have the fuel placed in our fireplaces and hearts, and then the oxygen applied through our speech. Here's a basic picture of how this works.

As we begin this life on earth, even as early as the time we spend in our mothers' womb, wood (fuel) begins to be stacked in our fireplaces (hearts) by those who have access to us. This includes our parents, other family members, teachers, entertainers, celebrities, politicians, news outlets, and anyone else who has access to speak into or over our lives or have actual physical contact. As we grow and can make decisions for ourselves, we begin to stack more wood (fuel) into our own lives through the choices we make with what we listen to, look at, allow to influence us, and even what we do with our bodies. At this point, wood or other junk is being stacked in our fireplace from many different sources.

This is significant because the fuel stacked in our fireplaces (hearts) determines how we think and view things. It shapes our perceptions and can establish strong thought patterns. This does not only include things that are said to us or words that we hear, but this also includes things like trauma from emotional abuse, physical abuse, sexual abuse, traumatic events we witness, our own sins, generational issues, and more. These all play a role in what kind of fuel is laid down in the fireplace of our hearts. This eventually begins to manifest in the way we speak, act, and react. Jesus said that a good man from the good treasure of the heart brings forth good things, and an evil man from the evil treasures of the heart brings forth evil things (Matthew 12:35; Luke 6:45).

Only the fuel of God's Word and things in line with the character of Christ Jesus will be used by the Holy Spirit to fuel the Fire of God. As we stack the fuel of God's Word in our hearts, it transforms the way we think. We fan those flames by breathing oxygen into them or by speaking and declaring the word. The Holy Spirit brings the heat, or power, to back God's Word and cause it to manifest with light, refining, purification, and more! Then we begin to fulfill our purpose on this earth: to advance His kingdom here on earth, be fruitful for His kingdom, and multiply the fruit for His kingdom.

The bad fires, the tormenting fires, are a direct result of all the other influences I listed in the two paragraphs above. For instance, trauma experienced as a child stacks junk or trash in our hearts that, as we grow, causes our thought patterns to get messed up. We then begin to struggle with issues like fear, rejection, guilt, shame, worthlessness, and more. This, in turn, manifests in our choices and the way we speak, act, and react. This combination of (1) heat from our souls and thought patterns, (2) fuel stacked in our hearts from the trauma, influences, and sins, and (3) oxygen breathed on it in the way we speak and declare words sparks a flame that begins to burn with a toxic fire in our lives.

What makes the toxic fires dangerous is that they can combine with many other toxic fires burning in us, and the results range from being nonproductive in life to being completely destructive to ourselves and those around us. All of this does not even include the works and influences of the demonic, which are only covered slightly in this book. However, the principles covered in this book will directly impact the access, influence, and power the devil does or does not have over you. When the Fire of God is burning in us, the enemy loses control and influence and loses all power over us.

In the next chapter, we'll uncover some truths that directly relate to how the enemy works in all of this process. Along with this will be the truth that there is no greater power than the power of Jesus! When the Holy Spirit dwells in you and is with you, victory is guaranteed through faith in Christ Jesus. We just need to surrender and trust in the complete work of Christ on the cross and the blood He shed for you and me—His way and His way alone!

# CHAPTER 5

# The Deception

THE THING ABOUT TOXIC OR TORMENTING FIRES is that, at first, the flicker can appear consistent with a standard fire being born. It will appear like everything is normal. But as it grows, the toxic portions of the fuel in the bed of our hearts begin to affect the way the fire manifests. These fires in us can operate similarly to the way natural fires work. Natural fires can manifest differently and will give us signals about the type of fire that's burning.

With natural fires, the more obvious signals are the possible differences in the color of the smoke or the possible differences in the odor of the burn. Who doesn't love the smell of clean, healthy wood burning at a campfire or in the comfort of a fireplace in the cabin? But smelling a stinky fire is usually more obvious to us, and toxic burns can produce any number of unpleasant smells. There are also possible differences in the color of the flames. For instance, natural gas can produce a different color flame than clean wood. Though the color of a gas fire might be pleasant to look at, it can serve as a warning that what is being burned is something far more dangerous.

Wood sometimes has that crackle and pop many of us enjoy at the campfire. But some materials that burn have the potential to manifest in dangerous explosions and popping that threaten everything around the fire. Then there are the silent effects of the toxic fire. The fumes and gases emitted into the air that you can't see. As it spreads, those who breathe it might not even know the silent killer they are breathing in.

But here's the problem: the deception is at the start of the fire, as it starts out small and seemingly harmless. Until it takes off, it can be hard to recognize the toxic elements of the fire. This same principle works with the toxic fires of sin burning in our lives. The enemy works hard to be deceptive and hide what is burning underneath, so we will not recognize it and, therefore, will not deal with it until, before you know it, the fire is burning hot and causing damage. This is the complete opposite of the Fire of God brought by the Holy Spirit, which always brings life, growth, and light.

The thing that makes it difficult to fight a natural fire is not just the heat. It's the smoke screen that it produces. The smoke can become so thick that it blocks out the light. It can bring confusion, disorient you, and even deceive you. Where's the actual fire? Where are the safe exits? Am I trapped in my doom, or is there a way out? This is one way the enemy uses the toxic materials fueling the fires of sin to produce a greater smoke screen. And when we are unaware of the truth, we can sometimes fan the flames with our own breath by speaking outside of God's truth. This only increases the flames and the smoke. Check out this truth again, spoken by Jesus:

> Make sure that the light you think you have
> is not actually darkness. (Luke 11:35 NLT)

So many of us have lived our lives through deception. Many live in a manner that mimics a true Christian walk and even puts off a little glow that makes them think it's the light (Fire) of God. But it's actually darkness because inside they are full of sin and darkness (Luke 11:44). More on this in the next chapter, but the remedy to this is to allow the Holy Spirit to bring the Fire and Light of Jesus to shine into your eyes and your heart, light up every dark place, and burn out the sin. This will produce a heart of light, integrity, and honesty (Psalm 25:21) that God can use for His kingdom.

The fires that burn in us that are not of God can either be hidden and seemingly silent or they can be loud and boisterous. The raging fire is significant because of the damage it causes. Fits of rage and violence, uncontrolled lusts, glaring hatred, and the like are usually obvious to those closest to the fire because the flames burn those around them in the way the fire manifests. But often, we have bad fires burning in our hearts that are not so obvious to us or those around us. It is hard to detect the flames, and what we see are the symptoms or the smoke. These symptoms, or smoke, can be as subtle as agitation, being easily offended, chronic sicknesses, anxieties, chronically failed relationships, and more. The only way to overcome this is to diagnose the situation and locate the fire so you can address it. However, you can only accomplish this with the help of the Holy Spirit.

The problem with deception is that it hides the truth. That's why it's deceptive. If you can't see, can't find, or can't diagnose the fires burning in your heart, you can't or won't deal with them. Or you will deal with them incorrectly. That is why the enemy works so hard to deceive you. He knows the truth will set you free (John 8:32).

These seemingly small issues (fires) burning in us can stay hidden for years. But behind the scenes, deep inside, they are growing, increasing, and multiplying until they either grow big enough to start causing significant damage, blow up into a raging fire, or someone turns on the true light of Jesus and exposes what's behind the smoke.

Just to recap from previous chapters, these bad or tormenting fires can be a number of ungodly things like anger, rage, pride, lust, jealousy, self-righteousness, envy, unforgiveness, bitterness, resentment, offense, guilt, shame, legalism, sexual immorality, fear, doubt, unbelief, cowardice, timidity, anxiety, being judgmental, a gossiper, hypocrisy, being a slanderer, boastful, covetousness, dishonoring to parents and those in authority, causing division, unfaithful, not dependable, filthy talk and communication, addictions of any type, idolatry, gluttony, and overindulgence…need we go on? The bottom line is that no matter how good you think you are, apart from the blood of Jesus, we are all guilty before the Lord and deserve punishment. It is by His grace that we are saved through faith in Jesus alone (Ephesians 2:8). This list of fires can go on, but when we are willing to let the Spirit of God assess us, we will find we continue to need His Fire to burn in us.

This issue of bad fires burning in us is like what I call "cockroaches in the kitchen." I've had the unfortunate experience of being in places where roaches were a real problem. I'm not talking about the occasional roach seen walking around. I'm talking about roaches acting like they are your roommates. If you know what I'm talking about, then this will make sense to you. What happens when you turn off all the lights and go to bed? Then in the middle of the night, you wake up thinking you want a glass of water or milk. You stumble through the dark, make your way to the kitchen, and flip on the light switch! Surprise! The cockroaches are having a party! Or a riot. And when the light comes on, they scatter. Gross, I know, but it's true.

This is how the enemy works. He is deceptive and tries to stay hidden in the dark. The darker it is in your heart, the more active the enemy is. That's those hidden, bad, or tormenting fires. You must allow the Holy Spirit to turn on the true Light to expose them. Surrender to Him and ask Him to create in you a clean heart and show you what's hidden so that you might address it with His help. He wants to partner with you. More details are in the next chapter. I know, I keep saying that.

There's a reason Peter instructed us to be vigilant: because our adversary, the devil, is walking around parading like a roaring lion, looking for someone who will grant him permission to devour them (1 Peter 5:8).

Now I don't want to spend any time giving any kind of credit to the devil. He is a defeated foe. However, it is important to recognize his strategies. The Bible says we are not ignorant of his schemes or devices (2 Corinthians 2:11). So I want to point out what Peter told us in the next verse after he instructed us to be vigilant. Peter said to stand firm against the devil and be strong in your faith (1 Peter 5:9)! James said if we submit to God and resist the devil, he will flee from us (James 4:7)!

I want to explore Paul's idea that we are not ignorant of the devil's schemes a little more. The Greek word used here for schemes or devices is *noema*. This simply means thoughts or evil purposes.

In other words, we know how the devil thinks. His thought process and evil purposes can be summed up in this verse spoken by Jesus Himself:

> The thief's purpose is to steal and kill and destroy. My purpose is to give them a rich and satisfying life. (John 10:10 NLT)

This is the thief's whole purpose, and I don't think those are necessarily three separate things the devil does randomly. I believe in this verse that Jesus was revealing to us the enemy's strategic three-step process.

Step one: the thief starts by trying to steal from us. He brings distractions to try and steal our time from the things of God, like prayer, reading our Bibles, and going to church. He tries to steal our integrity; our commitment to God and His kingdom; our intimacy with God; our understanding of the Father, the cross, and the blood of Jesus; and our confidence in our relationship with Jesus, ultimately stealing our joy and peace. He will try to steal our understanding of holiness, our finances, health, unity, and more. Pretty much anything we let him get away with. He does this through lies and deception to make us doubt God and His Word because he has no power unless we believe his lies and forfeit to him. He will even use scripture to accomplish this, like he did with Jesus (Matthew 4:3–11). That's why we *must* know God's Word and know the character of Christ and God as Father. For the unbeliever, the enemy simply steals their ability to see the light of the gospel by blinding their minds to the truth (2 Corinthians 4:4).

Step two: when the enemy can get away with stealing these things from us, we become vulnerable. He then moves in for the kill. He will try to kill our faith and trust in Jesus in the hopes of killing our relationship with Jesus. He'll even try to kill you physically through sickness, disease, injury, suicide, etc. But thanks be to God, through Jesus Christ our Lord, the enemy has been defeated!

Step three: the ultimate goal, the endgame of steps one and two, is to destroy us completely. Destroy our God-given purpose and destroy our lives for eternity.

Before discussing how the enemy tries to accomplish this three-step process, I want to clarify something. In the second half of that verse above, Jesus says this:

> My purpose is to give them a rich and satisfying life. (John 10:10b NLT)

Also, Paul talks about what Jesus did to the devil:

> Having disarmed principalities and powers, He made a public spectacle of them, triumphing over them in it. (Colossians 2:15 NKJV)

Also, Jesus speaking, said this:

> Behold, I give you the authority to trample on serpents and scorpions, and over all the power of the enemy, and nothing shall by any means hurt you. (Luke 10:19 NKJV)

So if you are in Christ, you need not be afraid of the devil. Just be aware of how he tries to work against you. In the process of stealing, killing, and destroying us, the enemy wants to make us slaves to sin (John 8:34), but thank God for the freedom found in Christ Jesus (John 8:36)!

I can't complete this chapter without making you aware of what these schemes of the enemy look like. This chapter is titled "The Deception." He is recognizable if the devil shows up in his true form, blatant evil. That's not deception. To deceive someone, you must present a counterfeit, a look-alike, or an imitation that makes you think it is the real thing. The Bible says the devil disguises himself as an angel of light (2 Corinthians 11:14).

Since the beginning, the devil has been working through deception in people's lives so he can work his three-step process. That's how he deceived Eve in the garden. I do not believe we are to focus on the devil or give him any place of recognition as one who can compare in any way to our God. But it is foolish not to recognize the consequences of surrendering to him.

So back to it. A part of the deception is in the devil imitating the things of God. This goes even beyond his twisting scripture. We lose sight of the fact that the schemes of the enemy can be quite complex. He has been practicing since the beginning of man. We *must* stay close to Jesus through prayer and walk in His Word and the power of the Holy Spirit to avoid this deception. If you feel like you are knowledgeable or spiritual enough on your own to avoid deception without the Holy Spirit's help, you only deceive yourself. Stay humble and surrender to the Holy Spirit!

In Exodus chapter 7, we see the story of Moses and Aaron going to Pharaoh at the command of God to demand that Pharaoh let the Israelites go. Now the Israelites had been in Egypt for some four hundred years, and God said it was time for them to be set free. I believe God is saying to you right now, *It is time to be set free!* When they met with Pharaoh, God told Moses to have Aaron throw down his staff as a sign to Pharaoh. So Aaron threw down his staff, and it turned into a snake. But Pharaoh's magicians threw down their staffs, and they became snakes as well. They imitated what God had done. Now none of this can happen without God's permission, but the enemy tried to intimidate Moses and Aaron and act like they had equal power. But the snake from Aaron's staff swallowed up the snakes from the magicians.

As this unfolded in Exodus, chapters 7 through 11, we saw ten different plagues come upon the Egyptians before Pharaoh finally let the Israelites go. What was interesting is that the first two plagues, the water in Egypt turning to blood and the plague of frogs, were also duplicated by Pharaoh's magicians, just like they did with the staffs becoming snakes. But after that, there were eight more plagues they could no longer duplicate. God said enough.

I don't claim to know how or why God allowed this to happen. But I do know that this is a clear picture of how the enemy tries to deceive us. He tries to act like he has power when he can only do what God allows or what we give him legal access to do through our sin or surrender. At some point, if we remain faithful and obedient to God as Moses and Aaron did and do not get afraid because it looks like the enemy is powerful, God will show himself to be the *only* power, and He will set you free and protect you!

*Note:* The first plagues being mimicked were not *mano a mano,* or hand-to-hand combat between God and the devil. No, the enemy only did what God allowed. The Lord God of Israel, as always, was up to something. Faith was growing in Moses and Aaron, and God's fame was being broadcast through His mighty works to both the Egyptians and the Israelites.

I believe this is a picture of how God often works in the life of someone who has become enslaved to the enemy. There is a call to "let my people go." When we say yes to him, there can sometimes be initial confusion and a lack of discernment as to what signs and manifestations are from God and what is not. This is because the enemy does not want to let you go. He doesn't want the tormenting fires to burn out. To deceive you, he will try to mimic God with what seem like spiritual signs that hold just enough partial truth to be deceiving. He'll even try to quote scriptures.

There are differing opinions and theological views about what the devil can do. Some things are clear in scripture, but some things are not. I'm not an expert in this area, but I believe the enemy attacks our thoughts and dreams, though he cannot read our thoughts beyond what he suggests to us. Only God knows the heart and thoughts of man (1 Kings 8:39). Psalm chapter 23 tells us that we walk through the valley of the shadow of death. The enemy and his lies are a shadow for the obedient believer, but if you surrender to him through sin, you give him and death legal rights (Romans 8:2) and room to work in your life. Paul warned us not to give place or room to the devil (Ephesians 4:27). Those rights can only be taken back through the blood of Jesus.

Sometimes dreams and negative thoughts are the product of our own stinking thinking. These can be mental strongholds that need to be torn down (2 Corinthians 10:4). The Bible even says there are divining spirits and dreamers, and we can even have dreams that we ourselves cause to be dreamed of (Jeremiah 29:8). When you have genuinely given your life in surrender to Jesus and repented, you belong to Jesus, not the devil. The devil will try to hold onto control in your mind, but God has given us tools to overcome this and stand in full freedom.

This is where it is absolutely vital that we dive into the Word of God, pray, develop a relationship with the Holy Spirit, get involved in fellowship with true believers, get accountability with church leaders, and do everything else the Word of God prescribes.

As we do this, we begin to distinguish between signs and voices from the enemy and the voice and signs from God. We begin to discern deception. It will get to the point where the enemy's lies, deceptions, and weaknesses are exposed, and the power of God is manifest! When this happens, you will come out of Egypt!

# CHAPTER 6

# What's Really Going On?

IF THE BED OF THE FIRES BURNING in your life was built with toxic materials, then you can try to add clean wood on top, but the core of the fire will still be toxic. You can try to throw water on it, snuff it out, use a fire extinguisher, etc. But the exact method of getting that toxic fire controlled and then ultimately extinguished varies greatly based on what's fueling it. Example: you don't throw water on a grease fire. (That's what Panic causes.)

Some of us know we have fires burning in our hearts that are the result of sins and ungodly junk that's been allowed in our lives. We know this because of the way the fire manifests. So we keep throwing all kinds of things on top of the toxic fires in our lives, trying to extinguish them, but we find it's not working. Some run to drugs or alcohol, some deeper into sexual immorality, some work long hours or try to stay busy, and some become very religious or legalistic, but all of these methods can be like throwing water on a grease fire. It doesn't extinguish it, but it can make it spread.

Then we wonder why the fire is still toxic or, even worse, is growing and becoming more dangerous. This manifests itself in many ways. It can manifest in anger, jealousy, bitterness, or destructive habits. It is only after identifying the toxic fuel (or fuels) that was put in the fireplace—your heart and mind—that you can take the Word of God and discover the method (God's way) needed to put it out. It is in accomplishing this that we are then able to clear out the fireplace and *immediately* (never leave the fireplace empty; it must always be burning for God) put clean wood (the Word of God) in our hearts and begin to burn clean again for the kingdom of heaven.

Then any trash thrown at the fire will burn off. Now we know that all fires, except the Fire of God, can have an element of toxicity depending on the trash thrown at them. And if we live in this world, there is always going to be trash that we must deal with. The key is that the foundational fuel in our hearts is clean and solid with God's Word, and the Fire of God burns bright and hot so that any trash thrown on top will be quickly burned off. It is equally key that the foundational fuel of God's Word *not* be mixed with toxic materials (sin) so that the negative effects outweigh the benefits of God's Word. If you begin to allow toxic junk to reenter by giving in to sin as a practice or being consistently disobedient to God, the Holy Spirit and His Fire will not share space with that sin or evil. We are subject to sin and mess up at times, and it is the Holy Spirit that refines us and helps us overcome, but blatant, persistent sin will have negative effects.

It is important to understand that there are biblical principles that apply to everyone if we want to see the promises of God fulfilled in our lives. For instance, we are all required to have faith, trust, and belief in Jesus (Romans 1:17; Galatians 3:11). Everyone is required to repent (Acts 17:30). Jesus is the only way to the Father (John 14:6). The Word of God is what renews our mind (Colossians 3:10; Ephesians 5:26). We must forgive others to be forgiven by God (Matthew 6:14–15). The greatest commandments are loving God with all of our heart, mind, soul, and strength and loving others as ourselves (Mark 12:29–31). These are God's conditions outlined in scripture.

However, there is no specific formula for the specific way God deals with all the various issues in our lives. God heals, but how He chooses to heal or deliver one person may not be exactly how He chooses to do it for someone else. We do know that if we meet His conditions outlined in scripture, He will do it. We don't understand all of God's ways or how He deals with us. Jesus once spit on a man's eyes, and he was healed (Mark 8:23). That doesn't mean spit then becomes the formula. The formula is that Jesus is the answer. The Holy Spirit is the power! But we can't say that God will always use specific methods for everyone. We can say that He will always stay in line with His own word. There are solid biblical principles, and it is important to find the root cause of our issues and address them biblically, trusting that when we meet God's conditions, the Holy Spirit will move for us.

I know, personally, that when going through my own battle with tormenting fear and anxiety, I would listen to various testimonies and sermons preached and would read books where people would say they had battled something similar to what I was going through at that time. They would say it lasted this many years, and then one day they read a particular verse in the Bible, and a light of revelation suddenly came on, and the fear suddenly lifted. I would then find myself trying to quote and memorize the same verse as them, only to find I was not getting the same results that person did. Why? Because that was not what God specifically had in mind for me. He knows our hearts and all our thoughts. He knows exactly what we need and the exact right time for it to happen. He knows the root causes. Some receive freedom, deliverance, breakthrough, or healing from suddenly having a verse revealed to them by the Holy Spirit. Some get it through the laying on of hands or prayers from others. Some receive deliverance from the demonic through deliverance ministries. Some receive it when they are baptized in water, and still others receive it through other sovereign acts of God.

The point is this: Do not put God in your box of thinking. Do not limit Him to what you think is the formula. He is God and has no limitations. We are mere humans with tremendous limitations. The key is meeting His conditions in the Word and then trusting. Trust Him. He alone is the answer. Jesus is the one who purchased our freedom on the cross. He knows everything about you and knows exactly what will work. And here is a *huge* key that you and I *must* grasp if we want to receive from the Lord. Here it is. Ready?

*It's not about you!*

I know that's a shocker. But it's true. We are His people, the sheep of His pasture. Everyone belongs to Him (Psalm 100:3; Psalm

24:1). We are created to fulfill God's purpose and to see the kingdom of God manifest here on earth (Matthew 6:10). The four gospels are full of parables Jesus taught, showing us that the will of the Father is for us to be servants for His Kingdom. We are to bear fruit and multiply through service to His kingdom. That is why we need to be free. When we can humbly and truly say that we surrender to His will, for His purpose, and for His glory, we have met one of the great conditions for freedom and deliverance.

So many of us bang our heads in frustration, wanting so badly to stop hurting, fearing, struggling, or whatever the problem is, that we focus on stopping the pain for our own relief and don't come to the point that the purpose for which we desire breakthrough is so that the name of Jesus will be glorified and the gospel preached. King David said, "He restores my soul; He leads me in the paths of righteousness for *His name's sake*" (Psalm 23:3 NKJV). David understood it was not about him. God restored and renewed David's soul so he could bring honor and glory to God. That the name of God would be made famous. It's about Him!

Okay, let's continue the topic of finding the specific root problems and dealing with them God's way. How do we make this practical? It starts with acknowledgment. You cannot confess sins, repent, forgive others, or fix any issue if you are not first willing to acknowledge there is a problem. You must, at the same time, acknowledge that you need God. Understanding that, on your own, apart from Christ, you are weak, wicked, and wanting will start you on the path of surrender. I know that sounds harsh, but it's the truth.

Pride and self-righteousness will not only keep toxic fires burning in you, but also depending on what is burning in your heart and mind, they could keep you from God's presence forever. It's a sobering thought, but Jesus paid too high a price for us not surrendering to His love.

Unfortunately, we tend not to work in prevention or self-evaluation very well. A good practice would be to examine ourselves (1 Corinthians 11:28) against the Word of God and see where we fall short or don't look like Jesus. What about our character does not look like the character of Christ? We should all be doing this, but we fall short in this area. I'm doing much better with this, but I also still must constantly remind myself of this discipline.

Even when we examine ourselves, only the Holy Spirit knows everything about us, even the deep things and the secret things of our hearts (Psalm 44:21; Acts 15:8). So to take it a step further, it is important that we be willing to allow the Holy Spirit to refine us, create in us a clean heart, renew our minds, and make our character more like Jesus. When we are willing to pray this and allow the Holy Spirit to work, we will find that tests and trials will begin to reveal what is really burning in our hearts.

As I mentioned before, character flaws will begin to surface, just like impurities come to the surface when you refine gold. You can't see the impurities until you heat up gold in the furnace. But once it is melted, the other metals and impurities float to the surface, and then you can scoop them away, leaving pure gold. But this can't happen without the fire.

This is the process we talked about in chapter 2, in which the consuming fire of the Holy Spirit burns out sins and impurities. This process of trials and tests will reveal the truth about what's in your heart. Will you maintain integrity? Will you cheat, take shortcuts or the easy way out, get angry, easily offended, lazy, prideful, resentful, mean, unfair, or have some other issue? Or will you recognize, acknowledge, and repent of what the Holy Spirit reveals to you so that your character will become more like Jesus? This process reveals the truth about us, and, again, Jesus said this about truth:

> And you shall know the truth, and the truth
> shall make you free. (John 8:32 NKJV)

We usually see this verse as pertaining only to the truth as being God's Word. In other words, when you get to know God's Word, His Word sets you free. This is absolutely correct, but I believe there's something deeper here. In chapter 5, we spoke about the deception of the enemy and how many are deceived and do not see the corruption burning inside (Luke 11:44).

Scripture tells us that the god of this world blinds the minds of those who are lost, so the light of the gospel of Christ can't shine unto them (2 Corinthians 4:4). Jesus, who is the Word of God, is the light that shines in the darkness (John 1:1–5). So when scripture says the truth sets us free, it includes the truth of His Word shining as a light in our hearts, exposing sin, darkness, and issues, and we come to know the truth about who we really are. So we know the truth about who God is, but we also come to know the truth about ourselves when examined against the Word of God. Once God reveals to us the truth about our own hearts and the truth of His Word, we can be set free! Now we can deal with stuff because the light is on.

# Extinguishing Toxic Fires

Now it's time to apply the correct principles to extinguish the toxic fires in our lives while fanning the flames of God's Fire in us! But before we explore this further, it is important to mention that sometimes we experience issues with our mental state or our physical health that are not necessarily the result of a spiritual issue. Sometimes these are the result of something organic or physical, such as a chemical imbalance. Sometimes it is the result of a combination of both spiritual and organic issues.

It is also important to remember that things like poor eating habits, poor sleeping habits, stress, overworking, not exercising, and other poor stewardship of our mind and body can have negative effects. I believe this is a sin as well because our bodies are the temple of the Holy Spirit (1 Corinthians 6:19), and we are God's creation. However, I'm pointing out that there are some things that can be addressed by simply adjusting our habits and routines or by seeking medical or other professional help.

However, this is not always the case, and we will address two major causes of toxic fires burning in us. The principles for dealing with these are biblical truths that apply to us across any issue we face. We will deal with these principles for addressing toxic fuels that fuel the fires caused by sins we commit and for those fires caused by victimization or sins that others commit against us.

*Sins committed*

First, understand that we have all sinned (Romans 3:23, 5:12), and if we claim we have not sinned, we deceive ourselves and are calling God a liar (1 John 1:8–10). That may sound harsh to you, but it is God's Word, and remember, the truth is what sets us free, and this process starts with acknowledging the truth.

When you are aware of sins or the Holy Spirit reveals sins in your heart, you must be willing to acknowledge those sins and go before God to confess. Don't be stubborn. When we try to cover our sins, ignore them, or hide them from God, we cannot prosper (Proverbs 28:13). In fact, King David tried that, and God sent the prophet Nathan to confront him about it well after David had committed adultery with Bathsheba and had her husband Uriah killed to cover it up (2 Samuel 11). David ended up writing Psalm chapter 51 in a heartfelt repentance for his sins after being confronted. We must understand that hidden and covered sin will bring destruction if not repented of. Achan was a man who sinned and covered it, and his sin affected the entire nation and ultimately cost Achan and his family their lives (Joshua 7). The Bible is full of stories that reveal the destructiveness of sin, and of course, the result of sin that is not repented of and covered by the blood of Jesus is death (James 1:15).

That said, understand that we now live under the new covenant. Christ Jesus shed His blood, gave His life, and paid for the sins of the entire world. Why would we not confess to Him and receive His grace and *total* forgiveness? "If we confess our sins, He is faithful and just to forgive us our sins and to cleanse us from all unrighteousness" (1 John 1:9). The Bible makes it clear that we have redemption through His blood (Colossians 1:14). Don't leave it in the darkness. Confess to the Lord and receive the cleansing blood of Jesus.

Another aspect of this principle is the importance of finding a trusted friend or spiritual leader and confessing to that person as well. It's not always wise to air out your dirty laundry to anyone and everyone or to post it all over social media. Find that person to confide in, and confess those sins and weaknesses. That believer can then pray for you that you might be healed (James 5:16). Bring it to the Light!

We covered this a bit in previous chapters, but remember that sin has no place in the life of the believer, and sin is no longer your nature. That must be your mindset. We are always subject to struggles, but Christ Jesus won the victory. Once we confess our sins and ask for forgiveness, we are forgiven! *But* we also need to renounce and forsake those sins (Proverbs 28:13). Remember what Jesus told the woman who was caught in the act of adultery? He told her that He did not condemn her but that she was to go her way and *sin no more* (John 8:11). In another place, Jesus healed a sick man next to the pool of Bethesda. He later found the man in the temple and told him, "Sin no more, lest a worse thing come upon you" (John 5:14b NKJV). Make up your mind to renounce and forsake those sins in all their forms.

This is where repentance comes in. The Bible instructs us to confess and repent of our sins (Matthew 4:17; Luke 13:3; Acts 2:38, 17:30). To *repent* means to change the way you think about sin. You literally turn toward God and His way of thinking about sin. You can reference chapter 1 again. But it looks something like this as an example: (Again, an example only.) *Father, I agree with you that sin is wrong and has no place in my life. I don't want it, and I refuse to allow it to dominate and control my life. I am guilty; no excuses; I won't justify it; no blaming anyone else. I confess my sins, and I ask for your forgiveness. Sin is not my present or my future, and it is not my nature. I have been resurrected with Christ in my new life. I renounce all sin from this day forward and turn my eyes toward you, Jesus, and I give you, Holy Spirit, full permission to work in me as I walk in freedom and new life in Jesus.* It can't just be a memorized prayer; it must literally be our new way of thinking.

Again, we live in a fallen world. If you are struggling with an area of sin, do not let the enemy bring condemnation. God will forgive the repentant sinner each time we come to Him (1 John 1:9; Matthew 18:21–22; Luke 17:4). But if you let the enemy deceive you into thinking you can blatantly persist in sin without consequence, you are headed for destruction (Romans 2:5). You are better than that. Don't let the enemy steal your God-given potential. You are a child of the one and only true God. He is your Father and loves you dearly. If you fall, confess it; get back up; turn from it; and keep going! Jesus paid too high a price for us not to walk in victory over sin.

*Key:* If someone has sinned against us, God requires that we forgive them if we expect God to forgive us. I'll cover this further below when we discuss being victimized, but it is also key to extinguishing toxic fires of sin.

Okay, so we established the need to acknowledge our sins, confess them to God and ask for His forgiveness, confess to someone you trust and have them pray for you, renounce and forsake the sins, walk in true repentance, and forgive others. I'll also add that restitution may be required in some cases. It could be going to the person you hurt or offended and asking them to forgive you, or maybe paying back the person you cheated out of money. Maybe you lied about someone and need to correct that lie to restore the person's reputation. Whatever the case is, I strongly encourage you to ask the Holy Spirit to lead you in this and seek godly counsel from trusted spiritual leaders before attempting restitution in any situation because every situation is unique and could hold issues requiring you to use wisdom and caution.

Tremendous progress is made at this point, but keep walking in the light. Another thing is to set boundaries and establish accountability. Jesus said that if your eye causes you to sin, pluck it out (Matthew 5:29). Now don't go pluck out your eye. Jesus was making a point, and to use a current example of this, if your computer causes you to be tempted by something like pornography, it's better to get rid of the computer than to keep falling into that sin.

Be open with those around you. Find someone you trust who can call you out on something they see you slipping into. Remember, if you feel the need to hide it, something is wrong. Your life is too precious to God not to do everything necessary to keep a smile on His face and keep the spirit of God feeling welcome and comfortable in your life.

Another issue to be keenly aware of is that when we participate in sin, the devil seeks to use it to gain access to us. It is very real that the enemy will use these open doors to harass and torment people. These torments could be anything from simply harassing us with temptations and lying thoughts to physical afflictions, significant mental strongholds (2 Corinthians 10:4), varying levels of torment, and strong demonic attachment and influence that require deliverance. I'll not debate the question of Christians being demonized, but I will say I believe that a Christian cannot be demon-possessed, as you belong to God through faith in Jesus, and the Holy Spirit lives in you.

However, do not give place to the enemy (Ephesians 4:27) to trap you and enslave you to demonic influence, torment, and sin. If you find yourself in this, do the things we've discussed in scripture. Confess, repent, renounce, forsake, forgive others, and get accountability. Then seek godly counsel from Spirit-filled believers and leaders about the possible need for deliverance and/or inner healing.

But the biggest key is to remember that it was Jesus who shed His blood, died, and was resurrected. It was Jesus who disarmed the devil and triumphed over him at the cross (Colossians 2:15). Victory only comes through your relationship with Him! When we confess, repent, and do these things, we are simply meeting His conditions and partnering with the Holy Spirit. The Holy Spirit brings the True Fire that extinguishes those bad, toxic, counterfeit fires. You can be free! You will be free!

Note: When you confess and repent of your sins, they are washed away by the blood of Jesus (1 John 1:7–9). God no longer remembers them (Isaiah 43:25; Hebrews 8:12). You are not your mistakes or failures. Your past is dead and gone. You are forgiven. Do not let the enemy constantly accuse you. Move forward. Go your way, and sin no more!

*Victimized*

Victimization is the other cause of toxic fires that can burn within us. We just discussed the issue of the sins we commit ourselves. Those are self-inflicted wounds. But the other major source of fuel for toxic fires comes from the junk that others deposit into our lives. This starts even before we are born and continues the entire time we are on this earth. The difficult thing is that we have little to no control over how others treat us or how they influence us when we are children. As we get older, we gain more control over outside influence but still do not have the ability to control everything others try to do to us. This highlights the importance of walking with the Lord so that He might be the help we need (reference Psalm chapter 91).

We'll look first at the influences that affect us as children. As I mentioned, this starts even before we are born. Our parents begin the process of shaping our lives and stacking wood in our hearts and minds that can later become the fuel for many of the toxic fires burning in us. Often, parents speak things over their children even as they are developing in their mother's womb, which is contrary to God's Word. Many parents do not realize the truth of Proverbs 18:21, which tells us that "Death and life are in the power of the tongue, and those who love it will eat its fruit" (NKJV). This verse applies to much more than just how parents speak over their children; it applies to everything. Could it be that your parents spoke words of rejection, resentment, or other words that were contrary to the life God desires for us all?

I'm not necessarily dealing with things like generational curses, bloodline curses, iniquities of our fathers, etc., in this book, but these are also real issues that the Holy Spirit will help you discover and deal with. It is important to remind us that Jesus paid for our freedom, and we have complete access to that freedom through faith in Jesus. Those curses are broken in Jesus's name. If you feel this might be an issue, seek godly counsel to address those things. You are saved if you genuinely give your life to Jesus and repent of your sins. You can renounce and reject every curse spoken to you by others. As you come into agreement with fellow believers and they pray for you, every curse will be broken by the blood of Jesus!

As you begin to develop as a child, your mind develops along with you. There are several influencers constantly depositing fuel in your heart and mind, developing the way you think. This is not an exhaustive list, but the influencers include your parents, other family members, friends, teachers, coaches, medical professionals, books, television, social media, movies, music, video games, and so much more. Each of these is stacking wood, or fuel, in your life. Here's the question: are they stacking clean wood from the Word of God, things pertaining to the kingdom of heaven, or are they stacking toxic materials like things pertaining to sin, defeat, or anything else that leads you away from God?

Let me take a moment to make sure we keep this in perspective. I don't want to make anyone feel discouraged by the overwhelming thought that there is so much negative speaking in our lives. How can we overcome it? Explore this verse with me:

> When His disciples heard *it,* they were greatly astonished, saying, "Who then can be saved?" But Jesus looked at *them* and said to them, "With men this is impossible, but with God all things are possible." (Matthew 19:25–26 NKJV)

When Jesus said this, He was responding to a question posed by His disciples. A rich man had just asked Jesus about what he needed to do to get into heaven. Jesus answered the man and eventually said that if he wanted to be perfect, he should sell everything and give it to the poor. The man went away sad because he was rich. This prompted Jesus to say that it was very hard for a rich man to enter the kingdom of heaven. In turn, the disciples asked, Who then can be saved? Jesus replied, With men, it is impossible, but with God, all things are possible. I brought this out to reveal the treasure of truth that is glaring at us in this scripture: *with God, all things are possible!* We live in a fallen world, and a lot is thrown at us, but we can overcome anything with *God.*

The fuel deposited in our lives comes not just from the words spoken to us but also from the things done to us. Countless children are victimized every day. We've all experienced some level of abuse or victimization in our lives, specifically as children. For some of us, it was as subtle as having a controlling parent or growing up in a home where God was not feared, and so it was acceptable to listen to or watch just about anything, even evil that was hidden in some types of music or other entertainment. For others, the abuse was not so subtle. Some experience things like significant verbal abuse, physical abuse, sexual abuse, or even a combination of all of these. There is so much more, including neglect, broken homes, no love in the home, parents who show favoritism, and more.

I spent many years working in a career where I had the unfortunate experience of seeing some of the most horrific abuses of children and people in general. The bottom line is that sin is destructive, and I believe most do not realize how destructive it can be. I am trying to make the point that if you have experienced anything like this, it is important to know you are not alone. The more significant the abuse, the more toxic the fuel that was placed in your life, and it is important to know that God did not do that. He gave men free will and choice. We live in a world that is fallen, and people make very bad choices that affect not just ourselves but also those around us. Though God did not cause the sin, He loved us enough to send a remedy in His son Jesus (John 3:16).

Even as adults, we deal with physical abuse, sexual abuse, control and manipulation, pain, attacks from others, etc. We experience being lied about, betrayed, stabbed in the back, cheated, verbally abused, and more. The point is that we all suffer from these things. Maybe not the exact same things, the exact same way, or to the same extent, but we all experience being victimized on some level.

The issue is that, whether it's as a child or an adult, these things can stack fuel in our minds that can lead to toxic fires burning in us. This toxic fuel comes in many forms and can manifest as fires of offense, unforgiveness, bitterness, resentment, fear, rejection, control, manipulation, emotional trauma, anxiety, depression, lust, anger, rage, hatred, lying, deception, self-righteousness, pride, legalism, religion, confusion, strife, division, jealousy, envy, addictions, and more.

When these things manifest in our lives because others deposit them through their words or actions against us, the remedy or method to extinguish the resulting fires is a bit different than the methods related to fires created by our own sins. However, the foundation is still the same. Jesus is the answer, and it requires the power of the Holy Spirit.

Remember the story about Lazarus, Jesus's friend, who died? After he had been dead for four days, Jesus arrived and raised him from the dead. But when Jesus called Lazarus to come out of the grave, the Bible says he came out, but his hands and feet were still bound in grave clothes, and his face was wrapped in a headcloth. So even though Lazarus was raised back to life, he was still bound up in grave clothes. Jesus then told those around Lazarus to unwrap, loose, and let him go (John 11:43–44). This is a picture of us as well. When we give our lives to Christ, we have new lives, but we often still have some old grave clothes wrapped around us that keep us bound in some areas. These are those toxic fires still burning. We need someone to loosen our grave clothes and let us go or unwrap us.

That process of being released from the results of victimization begins with acknowledging there's an issue. If you don't know the issue, ask the Holy Spirit to put His finger on it and show you. I listed above the many toxic fires we experience. If you're angry all the time, there's a reason. If you struggle with lust, there's a reason. If you are bitter, there's a reason. If you feel rejected and insecure, there's a reason. The solution could be as simple as changing the way you think, but it could be related to deeper issues from past trauma and hurt. It's not always the same reason for everyone, but everyone has a reason, and it is important that we let God put His finger on it so we can extinguish those fires and let the Fire of God burn in us. You'll have a difficult time loving God and others the way you should if toxic fires are allowed to continue burning.

After acknowledging the issues, ask the Holy Spirit to reveal the root cause. It might take counseling or some type of ministry to help you find it. Or you might already know where it came from. Maybe you were abused at some point, or perhaps you were betrayed by a friend you trusted. Either way, finding those root causes will lead you to address them, and here is the biggest area that needs to be addressed for those who, through victimization, have toxic fires burning: *forgiveness*. Yep, you must bring it to the light and forgive. Let it go. Not necessarily for the other person's sake, though it might help them too, but for your own sake.

First, if someone has sinned against us, God requires that we forgive them if we expect God to forgive us. If we are unwilling to forgive other people from our hearts for the sins they commit against us, then our heavenly Father will not forgive us (Matthew 6:12–15, 18:35; Mark 11:25–26). There are several good teachings out there about forgiveness. This is a huge issue in the lives of believers. So many Christians hold unforgiveness, bitterness, offense, resentment, and the like because of things others did to them. Please understand that holding these things inside opens a huge door for satan to work in our lives. It opens us up to deception and all kinds of bondage because, as the above-referenced scriptures tell us, God *will not* forgive us when we do not forgive others.

Don't let the devil trap you in this. True forgiveness is not just saying it, though that is part of it. Yes, confess forgiveness, but give up your right to see that person punished. Forgive them the way you want God to forgive you. Check your thoughts and attitude toward that person or those people. Is what you're feeling toward them something you would be okay with God feeling toward you when you ask Him to forgive you? Do you have a but at the end of your forgiveness? (I forgive you, but...)

If that person is unwilling to repent, they will have to answer to God. That's between them and God. But for your own sake, you want your heart to be clear before God. And (this is important), in some cases, it is not always possible to reconcile the relationship because it's not always safe or wise to allow that person any further access to you to harm or offend you again. You may have to set boundaries or break relationships altogether to avoid being hurt again. But the bottom line is to forgive. This is where the healing begins.

Another big issue I must address is the issue of offense. Are you easily offended? This is something I've battled with. The Holy Spirit has helped me, but since He began to deal with me, I've had to be intentional about recognizing, repenting, and dealing with it. If this is an issue for you, address it. Get help. Offenses lead to a lot of other issues. Getting offended easily shows we care too much about what people think about us, how we appear to others, and about being accepted by others. It shows we care too much about ourselves! When we get to the point where we care more about what God thinks, we are not so easily offended by the words or actions of others. If you do not deal with this, the enemy will use it to keep ugly feelings in your heart.

Offense can come from our own insecurities. Maybe we feel a need to be accepted. Whatever the root or the symptoms of the offense, we must deal with it. Offenses cause broken relationships. It has been the cause of a lot of church splits and people just leaving church. We get offended at the pastor, the worship leader, the usher, or the people in general. They didn't acknowledge me, or no one checked on me. We can go on, but please recognize the spirit of offense and don't let it dominate you. This will affect not only the church but also your job, family, friendships, and more. It can even subtly cause you to be easily offended by God. If it's there, acknowledge it and deal with it! Dealing with it means acknowledging it, confessing it to God, and following the truths outlined in the Word of God, many of which we cover in this book. Jesus made a way for our freedom from these things; dive into these truths and be free!

Going back to the story of Lazarus, another step is to get with fellow believers you can trust, and that you know walk with God, and have them pray for you and with you. Be wise about who you connect with, though; don't share your business with anyone, even if they call themselves Christians. Seek godly counsel from proven spiritual leaders, like your pastor, so these other believers can help you get free from the grave clothes! This might be in the form of professional Christian counseling, connecting with a Christian inner healing ministry or a deliverance ministry, or just getting plugged into a good group of solid Christians in a small group setting. Whatever path you take on this, be consistent, open, and honest, and most of all, know that these are all tools. But the answer is found completely in Christ Jesus, accomplished at the cross through His shed blood, and worked through the power of His Spirit! We will explore that power further in the next chapter. But before we do, I have an important notice below.

*To the one stacking wood*

One danger to the fireplace of our hearts is who has access to add to the wood pile or, worse yet, who can establish the base fuel. Some of this happens in our early years, and we can't control it. But as we grow older, it is imperative that we begin to manage, with God's help, who we allow access to our hearts, thus allowing the spirit of God to control what burns within us.

With this in mind, I want to switch gears for a moment and speak to you, not about the fires in your own life, but as someone who has access to add fuel to the lives of others. If you are a parent, a teacher, an entertainer, a counselor, a boss, a caretaker, a friend, a pastor, a youth leader, a spouse, or just about any other role we can think of, you are adding fuel to someone's fire(s). The question is, are you adding fuel that will burn toxic in their lives, or are you adding fuel from the things of God and His kingdom that will help them burn bright for Jesus?

Understand this: the things you say in the life of another person can have profound and lasting effects, especially on children. We have the potential to add toxic fuel with our words and actions, which can be devastating to the future of that person. If you are adding toxic junk to anyone's life, stop it! Stop speaking so negatively to them. Stop knocking them down. Stop abusing, stop controlling, stop manipulating, stop dominating, stop purposefully offending, and stop hurting people! Jesus came to give abundant life and to build up, not tear down. If you are damaging someone, stop it! Repent of it. We will all give account to God. It's time to repent and ask God for forgiveness. Ask that person to forgive you. Fix it.

I'm not telling you something that I haven't been guilty of myself. In fact, I believe we all violate this to some degree. It's diffi-cult, if not impossible, to have relationships with other people and not be guilty at some point of saying or doing something offensive or harmful to others. But when we invite the Holy Spirit to refine us, He will reveal to us when this is happening and give us the strength to fix it. However, I'll say it again: if you know you're doing this to someone, you don't need to wait for a revelation from God; just repent and stop it.

Remember, the Holy Spirit can use you to deposit the Word of God into people's lives. You can spread God's Fire to others and fan the flames of God in them. You can not only free yourself but also multiply that freedom in others. Build God's kingdom!

In closing this chapter, there is a saying my pastor says a lot. He may have gotten it from someone else, and you may have heard it. But the saying is, "Hurt people hurt people." This is usually why we make the mess we do to others. We have anger, irritability, or other issues that spill over into how we treat others. Getting ourselves free frees us up to be used by God to deposit the fruit of the Spirit into the lives of others, to build them up and to encourage them in the things of God. Always work to allow the Holy Spirit to work through you to leave people better than you found them. It will not be you who betters them; it will be the spirit of God in you. We just yield as a vessel, so the Fire of God will burn in those around us. Okay, now to the chapter I've been waiting for.

# CHAPTER 8

# True Fire!

WE HAVE SPENT A LOT OF TIME talking about all the toxic junk that burns in our lives as the result of man's sinful, fallen state. I pray that you have gained a clearer understanding of why you may have some of the struggles or issues you experience in life and some of the practical biblical steps to overcome them. But here's the most exciting part of this entire book: *it's all about Jesus!*

All those other fires we've talked about, the ones I called bad or toxic, are just imitations. They're not the real thing. They have real destructive consequences, but they are not the *True Fire!* The true fire comes from God alone and is a definite work of His spirit! We have access to His Fire through Jesus. The Father loved you and me so much that He gave His only Son, Jesus, to die for us and to give us everything we need for abundant life (John 3:16–17)—for a life that burns for Him!

We are truly living in the eleventh hour, and the enemy perpetrates a lot of deception against the church. Jesus told us to be careful in the last days so that no one deceives or misleads us. He said many would come saying they are the Christ, and unfortunately, many would fall for it (Matthew 24:4–5). Many have made their own image of Jesus into a false Christ who fits what they want Him to be instead of surrendering to the authentic Son of God as both Lord and Savior. Don't fall for this! Follow the Word of God. Let Jesus be Lord and follow the Holy Spirit in God's truth, not your own counterfeit truth. Jesus said, If you love me, keep my commandments (John 14:15).

Here's the bottom line: God has called us to be His own and live a full life sold out to His will, His kingdom, and His divine purpose for us on this earth. It is *not* His will for anyone to perish or be destroyed (2 Peter 3:9) or to live anything less than an abundant and free life—a life of repentance, a life of victory, a life of freedom. The Lord paid a *very high* price to accomplish this. He gave everything. He gave Himself. Jesus allowed Himself not just to be killed but crucified, scorned, mocked, ridiculed, spit on, beaten, tortured, and more by the very humans He was dying to save. And yet, right in the middle of the worst part of the pain and suffering, hanging on the cross, with blood still draining from His beaten, bruised, and torn body, Christ Jesus was able to look up to His Father in heaven and utter these words, "Father, forgive them, for they don't know what they are doing" (Luke 23:34 NLT). That was too expensive for us to live carelessly with our hearts. We must live with hearts that burn for Him! And we must protect that Fire at all costs! Why? Because He loves you. He really, really loves you.

Because the Lord loves us so much, He has given us many powerful promises in His Word. But there is one in particular I want to highlight at this point. In scripture, several names are given to God. These names describe who He is. I want to focus on this one for those of you fighting the battle to extinguish those toxic fires in your life.

*Jehovah Rapha*

> And said, "If you diligently heed the voice of the Lord your God and do what is right in His sight, give ear to His commandments and keep all His statutes, I will put none of the diseases on you which I have brought on the Egyptians. For I *am* the Lord who heals you." (Exodus 15:26 NKJV)

It's right there at the end of the verse: "I am the Lord who heals you." The original Hebrew words for Lord and heals are *Jehovah*

*Rapha*! Jehovah is the proper name for the God of Israel. It means the Lord, the self-existing One. The second name, *Rapha*, is translated to mean "to heal." This is correct, but there is more to the meaning of Rapha. Remember, God described Himself as Rapha. This name of God is most often used by the church when talking about physical healing. We say God is our physician, and He heals our bodies from sickness and disease. Again, this is true! *But* the word further means to heal the hurts of nations and to heal *individual or personal distresses.*

Why is this important? Well, it will make sense when you see the definition of the word *distress* and think about the topics in this book. The word *distress* means great pain, *anxiety*, or sorrow. It means acute physical *or mental suffering.* So when the Lord said He is the Lord who heals you, Jehovah Rapha, He was promising more than just physical healing. He was promising to heal you of that distress, that anxiety, that sorrow, and that mental suffering as well!

*But* look at the entire verse. We must meet God's conditions. We've discussed this in length in this book, and by the power of the Holy Spirit, you can do all things through Christ, who strengthens you (Philippians 4:13). Declare His name, Jehovah Rapha. He is the Lord who heals you! He will extinguish those toxic fires of anxiety, fear, and mental suffering!

As you rejoice over the Lord's promises, I want to share a few more essential principles for the heart that burns for Jesus.

## *The blood and the cross*

If it weren't for the blood that Jesus shed on the cross, the abundant life, forgiveness of sins, freedom, and everything else God has for us would be inaccessible. The blood Jesus shed was the ransom, the payment for your sins and mine. This is because blood is the life flow of the body. Life is in the blood (Leviticus 17:11). In the Old Testament, the blood of animals was used as a sacrifice to push back sins, but it could never fully satisfy the penalty of sins because the lifeblood of animals could not take the place of the lifeblood of humanity (Hebrews 10:4).

Justice dictates that the sin of humanity deserves the penalty of death (Romans 5:12, 6:23). That's the debt. Jesus came and gave His blood, His life flow, to pay for the sins of humanity. A perfect, sinless human life (blood) to pay the penalty for human sin (1 John 1:7; 1 Peter 1:19; Colossians 1:14; Ephesians 1:7; Romans 5:9). When we place our faith in Jesus Christ and the blood He shed, we are made right with God, and He frees us from the penalty of our sins (Romans 3:22–25, 8:2). We are no longer condemned to death because the just requirement of the law was satisfied, or paid for, by Jesus shedding His blood on the cross and dying in our place (Romans 8:1–2). Through the blood of Jesus, we are redeemed (purchased back), justified, made righteous, cleansed from all sin, delivered, set free, rescued, made complete, healed, and sanctified. It was all accomplished on the cross!

This is why Jesus is the only way to the Father. He is the Son of God. No one else lived a perfect life and then gave their life as payment for our sins. Jesus was obedient to the suffering of the cross on our behalf. Jesus, and Jesus alone, is the Way, the truth, and the life (John 14:6). I do not want to take for granted that everyone reading this book has made the decision to follow Jesus. If you have not made that decision, why not do it now? Or maybe you did at one point but have drifted away. Or maybe you've lived as a "Christian" but never really understood what true salvation was. Now is the time to make it a sure thing.

Make the conscious decision to believe in Him, give your life in surrender to Him, and receive the gift of life He gave through His blood on the cross, forgiveness of sins, and eternal life. It is that simple. You just need to believe it, confess it, and accept it. Confess your sins to God, ask Him to forgive you, and turn from those sins. The Bible tells us that if we confess with our mouths that Jesus is Lord and believe in our hearts that God raised Him from the dead, we will be saved because when we believe with our hearts, we are made right with God, and by confessing with our mouths, we are saved (Romans 10:9–10). At that moment, we step into His light and His life! We now have access to His Fire!

By the way, why did Jesus give His life and His blood? Because He loves you! Not because He had to. But because *He loves you!* A love that motivates that kind of action is a love you can trust, and it is a love that deserves to be loved back. If you just decided to accept and follow Jesus for the first time or to renew your relationship with Him, you need to tell someone.

*The power*

Here's another truth about true Fire: the power behind it doesn't come from us! We don't have to make it work. In fact, you can't make it work. There's nothing we can do to earn it or muster it up.

> So he answered and said to me: "This *is* the word of the Lord to Zerubbabel: 'Not by might nor by power, but by My Spirit,' Says the Lord of hosts." (Zechariah 4:6 NKJV)

That's where the power is. It's in the Holy Spirit. In an earlier chapter, we discussed the Holy Spirit's role in creation. He brings the power. He brings the Fire. He is the very spirit of God who gave the man Christ Jesus power to work miracles, set captives free, and preach the good news (Acts 10:38; Luke 4:18). The Holy Spirit was the power that raised Jesus from the dead (Romans 8:11). We must remember that the spirit of God is the one who brings True Fire and power to live the life that Jesus paid for. That's why Jesus instructed the disciples before He ascended to heaven.

> Behold, I send the Promise of My Father upon you; but tarry in the city of Jerusalem until you are endued with power from on high. (Luke 24:49 NKJV)

> But you shall receive power when the Holy Spirit has come upon you; and you shall be wit- nesses to Me in Jerusalem, and in all Judea and

Samaria, and to the end of the earth. (Acts 1:8 NKJV)

Remember this verse I quoted earlier in the book?

> I indeed baptize you with water unto repentance, but He who is coming after me is mightier than I, whose sandals I am not worthy to carry. He will baptize you with the Holy Spirit and fire. (Matthew 3:11 NKJV)

The Holy Spirit is not standing around, hoping you make it. If you struggle, perhaps He'll step in to help now and then. That might sound ridiculous, but that's how we live sometimes. We get frustrated with God and complain about why He is not helping us. The reality is that He is God, not us. He has all power; our lives are about His purpose and plan. Jesus instructed us to pray, "Your kingdom come. Your will be done on earth as *it is* in heaven" (Matthew 6:10). It's about the kingdom of God manifesting here on earth.

However, this requires that we partner with the Holy Spirit. Live a life of surrender and create an atmosphere where He is comfortable. When we repent of our sins, invite the Holy Spirit in, spend time fellowshipping with Him (2 Corinthians 13:14) in prayer and worship, and obey when He speaks to us, His Fire will burn in and through us. That Fire will burn with love for Jesus. It will burn with a revelation of the heart of the Father, burn us into alignment with the character of Jesus, burn in us with love for others, burn with fear and reverence for God and His holiness, and burn with power to manifest the kingdom of heaven right here on earth that others might believe in the Lord Jesus Christ and glorify God!

A key to this is understanding the importance of the Holy Spirit's presence. I can't adequately cover this topic in this book, but I felt like the Lord wanted me to include this very important message: *protect the presence!* It is so important that we not be irreverent to the Holy Spirit. The quickest way to offend Him is to persist in sin. But disobedience, distractions, bad attitudes, compromise with evil, and the like will offend Him.

Now the Holy Spirit is omnipresent, meaning He is everywhere at the same time and never leaves us (John 14:16). In fact, even when we sin, He is the one who convicts us, helps us straighten up, and guides us into truth (John 16:7–13). But His manifest presence, where He shows up and manifests His power and glory in some tangible way, is very sensitive. Keep your heart and life clean, be obedient, and respect Him. He is the very spirit of God! He is the third person of the Godhead, not some little flame or little god off to the side. He brings Fire and power. So remember, protect the presence. The Holy Spirit will manifest where He is respected and welcomed.

By the way, if you have not received the baptism of the Holy Spirit with the evidence of speaking in tongues, you can receive Him right now! Yes, when you become a Christian, the Holy Spirit dwells in you, but you need to receive the baptism recorded in the Book of Acts. He wants to clothe you with the power to be a witness through preaching, signs, and wonders, so many will come to know Jesus! And the gift of praying in tongues is invaluable to the believer. Don't wait; receive Him today!

Again, you don't have to make the Fire and power happen; He does it! Jump in the river and flow with His program. He will lead you. There is so much more to who the Holy Spirit is, but if you yield to Him, you will get a deeper revelation of the Father, the Son, and the Holy Spirit.

*The word!*

We can never walk with the Fire of God if we do not study the Word of God. In fact, part of the Holy Spirit's role is to guide us in all truth (John 16:13) and to remind us of the truth (John 14:26). Jesus called the Holy Spirit the Spirit of truth. The Holy Spirit will never speak or work outside of the Word of God (Galatians 1:8–9). If you want to avoid being deceived and know the will of God or the heart of God, learn the Word.

Like the other topics, I could never adequately cover the power and importance of the Word of God in this book. I feel my mandate is to provide a foundation for you to build on. So I will provide key scriptures and points about the Word from the Word. You can study deeper from there. Jesus said this:

> It is the Spirit who gives life; the flesh prof-its nothing. The words that I speak to you are spirit, and *they* are life. (John 6:63 NKJV)

Remember, the Holy Spirit is the power that brings the Fire of life. He does this through the Word, Jesus (John 1:14). If you want the spirit of life to work and manifest through you, you must get to know the Word, the gospel. Our human efforts accomplish noth-ing without partnering with the Holy Spirit and following His lead through the Word.

> For the word of God *is* living and powerful, and sharper than any two-edged sword, pierc-ing even to the division of soul and spirit, and of joints and marrow, and is a discerner of the thoughts and intents of the heart. (Hebrews 4:12 NKJV)

There are a few things I want to point out in this verse. First, the Word is living and powerful. Remember, it was the word that the Holy Spirit responded to when God created the world. The Holy Spirit was resting over the face of the deep, and then God *said*. As soon as the word came forth from God, the Holy Spirit was the power that created, bringing forth life from the spoken word. The word will bring life and power when we learn, speak, and apply it.

The second thing I want to point out is that the word divides between soul and spirit. This is key to distinguishing between the voices speaking to us. Examined against the Word of God, we can more accurately discern between our own thoughts in our mind (soul) and the voice of the Holy Spirit speaking to our spirit. This also applies to discerning the voice of the enemy.

Thirdly, pay attention to the last phrase. The word is a discerner of the thoughts and intents of the heart. Staying in line with the topic of this book, the heart is where the Fire of God should be burning, and the mind plays host to many toxic fires burning in us. When we look to diagnose what fires are burning in us, we must weigh everything against the Word of God. That's the mirror that will reflect back to us what's really burning inside. If we do not know the Word of God, we will misdiagnose the thoughts and intents of our hearts and live in deception.

> That He might sanctify and cleanse her with
> the washing of water by the word. (Ephesians
> 5:26 NKJV)

The spoken word of God is living water that cleanses and sanctifies our thought life daily. Through it, our minds are renewed as we begin to think more like He thinks.

> Your word I have hidden in my heart, That I
> might not sin against You. (Psalm 119:11 NKJV)

> All Scripture is inspired by God and is use-
> ful to teach us what is true and to make us realize
> what is wrong in our lives. It corrects us when
> we are wrong and teaches us to do what is right.
> God uses it to prepare and equip his people to
> do every good work. (2 Timothy 3:16–17 NLT)

When hidden in our hearts, the Word of God helps keep us from sinning against God, and when we do sin, it brings correction. As we learn more about His character and the heart of God, our hearts are filled with knowledge of Him, we separate ourselves from the sins that used to hold us captive, and we mature in Him. However, just memorizing scripture does not necessarily get it into our hearts. We must mix study with relationships and action. We spend time in prayer, fellowship with the Holy Spirit, and do the Word, or live it. This causes it to become a part of us as it sinks deep into our hearts.

> Your word *is* a lamp to my feet and a light to
> my path. (Psalm 119:105 NKJV)

The Word of God brings direction. This is the number one method God uses to speak to us: through His Word. The Holy Spirit will never contradict the Word of God. The answers we need can usually be either directly answered in Scripture or will be answered in the context of God's character as seen through Scripture. For instance, if I want to know if it is important for me to love God and others, there's scripture that directly tells me the greatest commandments are to love God with all my heart, mind, soul, and strength and to love my neighbor as myself (Mark 12:29–31). But if I am facing something for which there's no direct verse to give a specific answer, I can judge through the Word and wisdom and ask how my decision will stack up against the character of God as shown in His Word. I can check my motives in my decisions. Is my decision being made to bring glory to the Lord?

Let's get even narrower. Do I buy this house? You're not going to find a verse that says, "Yes, buy the brown house on Prosperity St." But scripture does say if we acknowledge the Lord in all our ways, He will direct our paths (Proverbs 3:6). I know I am to be a good steward of my finances. If my intention is to buy the larger house that I can't really afford just so I can make my neighbors jealous or to prove something to others, then I have a pretty good idea that I'm not making a choice in line with the character of God as shown in His Word. The bottom line is that the Word of God will direct you if you learn it.

> In the beginning was the Word, and the
> Word was with God, and the Word was God. He
> was in the beginning with God. All things were

made through Him, and without Him nothing
was made that was made. In Him was life, and
the life was the light of men. And the light shines
in the darkness, and the darkness did not com-
prehend it. (John 1:1–5 NKJV)

There's so much more we can say about the Word. The bottom
line is that everything was created by the Word, and the Word brings
life and light. The Word is the fuel that the Holy Spirit will use to
burn the Fire of God in us if we surrender to Him. As a reminder, if
we want to fan the flames of the Fire of God in our hearts, we must
breathe the Word! And you can't breathe or speak it if you don't know
it!

*More about God*

I heard a message from a famous preacher once, and he made
a statement that stuck with me. He was quoting another preacher,
I believe. Maybe you've heard this. I know I don't have it exactly as
originally said, but I think you'll understand. The preacher said, in
essence, that discovering God is like discovering water. You first discover God as a single drop of rainwater. Then as the raindrop enters
the small stream, joins with more water, and begins to flow, you discover more about Him. Then you think you've discovered all there is,
just to find the stream, which then flows into a river full of flowing
water, and you discover so much more about Him. You then think,
*Surely, I've got God figured out*, only to find the river meets with other
rivers, and they all flow into vast oceans of water that spread farther
than the eye can see, only to realize that's how big God is. His ways
are past finding out (Job 9:10; Romans 11:33).

So it's no surprise that we haven't scratched the surface of revealing the character of God or the power of His Fire that He desires to
burn in each of us. In my humble attempt, I remind myself, along
with you, that the God of all creation, the Almighty, wants to have a
relationship with me and you. Yes, He is holy, as we covered in chapter 1. Please *never* forget the reverent fear and awe of God. The one

and only true God. Maker of heaven and earth. But remember, He is just as much love as He is holy.

We've also covered several places that point out the power of God. But I want to remind you of His love, mercy, and grace. You can read the book of Psalms and quickly discover that David and the other writers of Psalms understood the character and heart of God. The writings describe God as loving, compassionate, merciful, full of grace, and loving-kindness. His love is described as unfailing (mercy). His mercy endures forever and is new every morning. He is rich in mercy. The writers also point out that this side of God is faithfully poured out to those who fear Him (Psalm 60:4, 103:17).

This is the whole purpose of this book: for you and me to discover that God wants to be our Father. He longs to have a relationship with us. But because He is holy, sin cannot be in His presence. So He remedied that by sending Jesus to pay for our sins so that we might repent, be in the right standing, and walk in a relationship with Him. He is a loving Father. The one who leaves the ninety-nine to go after the one lost sheep, the one who diligently seeks the one lost silver coin, and the Father who wholeheartedly accepts and embraces the prodigal son who finally returns home (Luke chapter 15).

Since we are discussing fire in this book, I want to relate this to camping with your father. If you have never had that, don't worry. I haven't either. At least not with a father. But I've watched enough old TV shows to know how it's supposed to work.

The father's role is to teach his child about the great outdoors. Part of any good camping trip is always a good ole campfire. The campfire serves many purposes. It's usually pleasant to just look at, smell, and listen to. Some, including me, find the crackle of the fire to be quite relaxing. The fire is a source of heat, keeping all the crowds around nice and toasty when the sun goes down. It can be a source of safety, warning bears and other creatures to stay away. The campfire serves as a tool for roasting hot dogs and marshmallows, making s'mores, or cooking the fish you caught earlier in the day. It's a great place to sit, talk, and tell stories.

The idea is that the father establishes the environment and teaches the benefits of the fire. He places boundaries, warns of the dangers, and ensures the safety of those around that fire. He creates an environment for the benefit of his family and harnesses the power of the fire he created to be used as a tool to make the camping trip a success.

This is what God is saying to us in this book. He's the Father sitting around the fire with us, teaching us the benefits of His Fire burning in us and the dangers of toxic, uncontrolled fires. Our journey on this earth is just a camping trip. It's temporary. Our real home is in heaven forever. If we follow the Holy Spirit's lead, our camping trip will succeed, and many will benefit from the Fire. So don't leave a dangerous fire that burns the forest when you leave. Let God's Fire burn in your heart and change the world for Jesus!

Remember, it's all about Him. Jesus prayed, "Your will be done on earth as it is in Heaven" (Matthew 6:10). In Psalm 23:3, David said that the shepherd leads us in the paths of righteousness, *for His name's sake*, or other translations say, to bring honor to His name.

# CHAPTER 9

# Maintaining the Fire

One last exhortation.

Any fire that is not maintained will eventually burn out. In chapter 3, we outlined the three elements needed for fire to exist: heat, fuel, and oxygen. All three of these must be maintained to keep a fire burning. It's the same with the Fire of God. Once His Fire is burning in you, He'll bring the heat and even supply the oxygen when we breathe the Word of God into it. But what causes most fires to die out is a lack of fuel. You must keep logs on the fire. The challenge to this task is that the enemy is busy bringing distractions that lead us away from our duty to maintain the Fire of God. We get too busy, and our relationship with the Father is usually the first thing to suffer.

It is essential that we stay in the Word, stay in prayer and fasting, continue to worship Jesus, stay in church, continue to give, and cultivate quality time in fellowship with the Holy Spirit. Stay in love with the Father. These are things that keep logs on the fire. They supply the fuel to maintain the Fire of the Holy Spirit. If the Fire begins to die out, the light grows dim, and the heat dies, taking us from hot to lukewarm and eventually to cold. Sin finds a hiding place in the resulting darkness as the light grows dim. The imitation toxic fires then begin to grow again, which is a place we do not want to be.

I want to leave you with a few final keys to avoid this dimming and help you maintain the Fire of God. I believe these are essential for the believer, and I pray they will help you keep the Fire of God burning bright in your life. These are by no means all the keys. There is so much more to our walk with God; we are all different, with different strengths and weaknesses. The important thing is that you build the defenses through the Word of God (Psalm 91:4) and partner with the Holy Spirit to keep the Fire burning.

*Prayer and worship*

There is no greater key to maintaining your relationship with God than the instruction given in the following verse:

> Never stop praying. (1 Thessalonians 5:17 NLT)

I honestly struggle trying to tackle this subject in such a limited way. Entire books are written about prayer. I have to remind myself that the goal of this book is to help believers diagnose what's burning inside so we can properly align ourselves with God's plan, burn with His Fire, and set the world on fire for Jesus in this eleventh hour!

To keep it simple, to pray is to communicate with God. Yes, prayer has many components, and it is important to learn how to pray. But I want to point out what we call the Lord's Prayer, or the example Jesus gave the disciples regarding how to pray because it gives us a beautiful picture of how to communicate with the Father.

> In this manner, therefore, pray: Our Father in heaven, Hallowed be Your name. Your kingdom come. Your will be done on earth as *it is* in heaven. Give us this day our daily bread. And forgive us our debts, As we forgive our debtors. And do not lead us into temptation, but deliver us from the evil one. For Yours is the kingdom and the power and the glory forever. Amen. (Matthew 6:9–13 NKJV)

I suggest a deeper study of this example He gave us, but the first key is that Jesus showed us how to approach our Father when we pray to Him. I know there are those who will say, *Just talk to God like He's your friend.* I believe there is some truth to understanding that aspect of our relationship as you get to know Him. However, I see a different approach often shown by those in scripture and by Jesus's own example here. Go back to what we discussed in chapter 1. We must always maintain reverent fear, respect, and awe of God. Recognize Him as your Father who loves you, but never lose sight of the fact that you are approaching the Almighty King, Creator of heaven and earth, the Holy One! This should actually help you enter His presence as you start your prayer time, pondering how great and awesome your heavenly Father is.

I wanted to highlight the second part of the prayer, asking the Father for His kingdom to come and His will to be done on earth as it is in heaven. In other words, we want to align our prayers with His will to see heaven manifest here on earth. It's all about God's plan and His kingdom manifesting here.

Then we move into talking to God about our needs, the needs of others, repentance, forgiveness, and everything else we might need to speak to Him about. No fancy words are needed. Just communicate with Him. I would like you to notice that Jesus ended the prayer with the same respect for His Father that He started the prayer with. He recognized that the kingdom, power, and glory belonged to God. Here are a few more verses on prayer:

> Confess your sins to each other and pray for each other so that you may be healed. The earnest prayer of a righteous person has great power and produces wonderful results. (James 5:16 NLT)

> Pray in the Spirit at all times and on every occasion. Stay alert and be persistent in your prayers for all believers everywhere. (Ephesians 6:18 NLT)

> One day Jesus told his disciples a story to
> show that they should always pray and never give
> up. (Luke 18:1 NLT)

> Keep alert at all times. And pray that you
> might be strong enough to escape these coming
> horrors and stand before the Son of Man. (Luke
> 21:36 NLT)

We will never get anywhere without prayer. A lack of prayer makes you vulnerable to attack and weakens your relationship with Jesus. The verses above show us that we must stay alert in prayer. Be persistent. Have you heard the saying, Little prayer, little power; more prayer, more power? The reason that is true is because prayer is a part of the relationship with the one who has *all power*. So if I'm not communicating with Him and maintaining a relationship, I cannot access His power. He knows all things, is everywhere, and has all power. Why would I not stay close to a Father like that? Also, remember that prayer is talking to God and listening to Him. Take time to be silent before Him. Listen. He will speak to you.

Finally, *worship*. This is more than just a component of prayer. It's more than singing worship songs at church. Worship is a heart connection with Jesus. Pour out your affection to Him. I believe any time you pour your affection to Him it is worship. It can be through song, giving, time spent in silence, heartfelt love for Him, or any form of adoration shown for Jesus that comes from the heart. The important thing is that He loves to be worshiped and will always respond to genuine, heartfelt worship.

> For God is Spirit, so those who worship him
> must worship in spirit and in truth. (John 4:24
> NLT)

True worship requires love and humility. It's not staying busy doing religious stuff. It comes from a heart that follows John 3:30: "He must increase, but I must decrease" (NKJV). When we are willing to lay our own crowns down at Jesus's feet and crown Him Lord, we move into a realm of heartfelt adoration for the King. There will be times when we don't "feel it" but press in and worship anyway. Don't go by feelings. If you invite Him, the Holy Spirit will lead your heart into love for Jesus (2 Thessalonians 3:5 and Romans 5:5).

Apart from sin, one of the biggest hindrances to our worship is distraction. We can get so busy with life that we miss the precious moments we can spend with our Lord, who is and has the answer to everything we need. If we are not careful, even the good we try to do can get in the way of the valuable time we should spend sitting at His feet. Read this passage of scripture and ask yourself, Are you Mary in this story, or are you Martha?

> As Jesus and the disciples continued on their way to Jerusalem, they came to a certain village where a woman named Martha welcomed him into her home. Her sister, Mary, sat at the Lord's feet, listening to what he taught. But Martha was distracted by the big dinner she was preparing. She came to Jesus and said, "Lord, doesn't it seem unfair to you that my sister just sits here while I do all the work? Tell her to come and help me." But the Lord said to her, "My dear Martha, you are worried and upset over all these details! There is only one thing worth being concerned about. Mary has discovered it, and it will not be taken away from her." (Luke 10:38–42 NLT)

It seems that there is a parallel here with the story of Cain and Abel from Genesis chapter 4. Cain presented an offering to God that was a product of his labor. It was the fruit of the ground, which he prepared with his efforts, and God did not accept it. Abel presented God with the best of the firstborn lambs from his flock. God accepted Abel's gift. There are different teachings about why God did not receive Cain's sacrifice, but I believe this is another picture, just like Mary and Martha, that shows the Lord is more concerned with the position of your heart than the results of your efforts. When we love God, we should work for His kingdom. But the key is that it's *His* kingdom. God is not as interested in your presumptuous efforts, even when they are considered "good," as He is in your obedience. Through our worship and time with Jesus, we are positioned to hear His heart and be led by the Holy Spirit. In these times of worship, we receive direction and clarity from the scriptures. This positions us to do what He wants instead of what we think He wants. Get the heart of God through genuine worship, then work.

*Accountability and community*

It is a dangerous place to be when you float out on your own with no connection or accountability. We need to have people we can talk to, confide in, and who can check on us. We need people who give us permission to call us out if needed. Find that person or those people immediately. That can't wait. (But *please* make sure they are trustworthy believers and not gossipers, backbiters, or people who give drama.)

Don't be a lone ranger; you're not that strong. Also, remember that who you hang out with will influence your behavior. Stay connected with a community of believers. Do not fall for the deception that you don't need other people in Christ. Beware of the spirit of offense that will try to creep in and cause you to be offended at some of the dumb things even Christians do. Forgive others the way you want Jesus to forgive you. Show grace to others for their faults, or what you perceive to be their faults. Let the love of God shine through you. This doesn't mean we can't be around unbelievers. God forbid, we associate only with Christians. We are called to evangelize the world with the gospel and bring the kingdom of heaven to earth for those around us.

*Keep everything open and in the light*

Why do businesses, and now just about every home, use security cameras? It's in the title: security. Though they are not a guarantee to stop crime, security cameras bring security against evildoers. You'll notice that people who walk on the property, knowing there are cameras but having nothing to hide, are not worried about being seen. They don't cover their faces or try to hide. But when you see someone in the camera covering their face or trying to hide from the camera, it's a pretty good indicator that something unsavory is afoot.

Why do we have security lights? You guessed it: for security. Again, it doesn't stop everything, but bad stuff likes to hide in the dark. When the lights are on, even the roaches will run and hide. If you have things you need to hide in your life, like on your cell phone, it's a good indicator you're into something you shouldn't be. There's no reason your spouse shouldn't be able to look at anything and everything on your phone, laptop, or wherever. Share your passwords. Uh-oh, some of you are getting uncomfortable. If your wife or husband lost or damaged their phone, would you be willing to let them use yours for the day? Without putting parental controls or special locks on certain apps? If not, why? The answer to that question will reveal a lot.

Again, I feel the need to warn you that not everything should be said or exposed to just anyone and everyone. But everything should be confessed and made open to God. Never try to hide anything from God. But when it comes to people, it's vital that you find trusted spiritual leaders or trusted, proven godly friends to confide in and confess to. It's not wise to spread your own dirty laundry to everyone. You open yourself up to being hurt and possibly hurting others unnecessarily. Seek godly counsel, and let the Holy Spirit lead you to when and to whom you should confess or share hidden things. Just remember to involve God and trusted people.

### Don't be presumptuous, be obedient

To *presume* is to take something for granted or to assume something. It also means doing something without the right to do it or permission. Presumption is a sin, and it got people in trouble in the Bible. I touched on this briefly above in relation to our worship. King

David knew the dangers of presumption, as he wrote about it in one of his many Psalms:

> Keep back Your servant also from presumptuous *sins;* Let them not have dominion over me. Then I shall be blameless, And I shall be innocent of great transgression. (Psalm 19:13 NKJV)

There are Bible translations that do not use the word presumptuous here. They use words like deliberate. However, the original Hebrew word here was *zed*, which means to be arrogant, proud, or presumptuous. In other words, David asked the Lord to keep him from the sin of being driven by pride and arrogance to act based on what he presumed to be the right thing instead of being humble and waiting to do what God asked of him.

There is a well-known story in 1 Samuel, chapter 15, where the prophet Samuel instructed King Saul to attack the Amalekites. Saul was instructed to completely destroy them for the evil they had previously committed against Israel. He was told to destroy everything and kill everyone, including their animals, and not to spare them. But King Saul assumed he knew what was right and did what God had not given him permission to do.

Saul attacked the Amalekites as instructed and destroyed all the people, but he spared their king, Agag, and kept all the best animals and everything else that appealed to them. When Saul was confronted about not completely obeying God's instructions to destroy everyone and everything, Saul replied by saying that they kept the best animals to make a sacrifice to the Lord. Sounds like a good reason, right? Part of the prophet Samuel's reply to Saul was that it is better to obey God than to offer sacrifice, and rebellion is like the sin of witchcraft, and stubbornness is like the sin of idolatry. I believe this disobedience directly resulted from Saul's pride, causing him to presume he knew best. As a result, God rejected Saul as king.

Here's the message: do it God's way and be obedient. It requires that we be humble and seek the leadership of the Holy Spirit. When pride dictates that you know what's best, you'll try to do things your way, according to what you think is best, instead of being obedient to the Lord. Being presumptuous will only cause you trouble and mess things up. Just because something seems good does not always mean that it is from God. He has a perfect plan and asks us to listen to His leading. The Lord has divine appointments for you. There are people to be reached with the gospel, and God knows the right time, method, and circumstances. We must be prepared to do it His way and in His timing because, again, He always has a plan, and His plan is perfect. So surrender and obey. Remember, God really, really loves you. His way is always for your best.

*Walk in love*

Dear friends, let us continue to love one another, for love comes from God. Anyone who loves is a child of God and knows God. But anyone who does not love does not know God, for God is love. God showed how much he loved us by sending his one and only Son into the world so that we might have eternal life through him. This is real love—not that we loved God, but that he loved us and sent his Son as a sacrifice to take away our sins. Dear friends, since God loved us that much, we surely ought to love each other. No one has ever seen God. But if we love each other, God lives in us, and his love is brought to full expression in us. And God has given us his Spirit as proof that we live in him and he in us. Furthermore, we have seen with our own eyes and now testify that the Father sent his Son to be the Savior of the world. All who declare that Jesus is the Son of God have God living in them, and they live in God. We know how much God loves us, and we have put our trust in his love. God is love, and all who live in love live in God, and God lives in them. And as we live in God, our love grows more perfect. So we will not be afraid on the day of judgment, but we can face him with confidence because we live like Jesus here in this world. Such love has no fear, because perfect love expels all fear. If we are afraid, it is for fear of punishment, and this shows that we have not fully experienced his perfect love. We love each other because he loved us first. If someone says, "I love God," but hates a fellow believer, that person is a liar; for if we don't love people we can see, how can we love God, whom we cannot see? And he has given us this command: Those who love God must also love their fellow believers. (1 John 4:7–21 NLT)

Amen!

*Fan the flames*

I'm writing to encourage you to fan into a flame and rekindle the fire of the spiritual gift God imparted to you when I laid my hands upon you. For God will never give you the spirit of fear, but the Holy Spirit who gives you mighty power, love, and self-control. (2 Timothy 1:6–7 TPT)

In this letter, Paul wrote to Timothy, exhorting him to stir up the gifts in him or, as *The Passion Translation* more clearly puts it, fan into a flame and rekindle the fire! Notice that Timothy has the responsibility to fan and rekindle. The Holy Spirit will bring the fire, but we are responsible for fanning the flames by speaking His Word! But remember, just like you can fan the flames, you can also extinguish the flames in your own life.

Never restrain or put out the fire of the Holy Spirit. (1 Thessalonians 5:19 TPT)

Interestingly, the original Greek word translated in this verse as *restrain*, was *sbennymi*, which can literally be translated as extinguish or quench a fire or things on fire. Though we could never put out the Fire of God in general, it is possible to grieve the Holy Spirit, and the result can be a loss of His Fire burning in us. I've more than covered this in the previous chapters, but please don't lose sight of this. Fan the flames every day. Follow these principles, and never let the fire die out.

*A final scripture*

> Meanwhile, the fire on the altar must be kept burning; it must never go out. Each morning the priest will add fresh wood to the fire and arrange the burnt offering on it. He will then burn the fat of the peace offerings on it. Remember, the fire must be kept burning on the altar at all times. It must never go out. (Leviticus 6:12–13 NLT)

It is our responsibility to be good stewards of God's Fire. Remember, the Holy Spirit brings the Fire. It is His Fire, not ours. You and I must daily maintain the altar of our hearts so that only the true Fire of God will burn and never go out!

My prayer for this world, our nation, the church, and for you is that we would experience a revival of repentance, a revival of the fear of the Lord, and a fresh Fire of the Holy Spirit for this, the eleventh hour! That we would carry the gospel with a demonstration of His power! With signs, wonders, healing, deliverance, and so much more demonstrated to the world, Jesus, and Jesus alone, would be made famous!

So stack on the wood! Burn bright! Burn hot! Burn well! Share the Fire with someone, and let the Holy Spirit use you to light the world on Fire for Jesus!

CRAIG YANCY GREW UP IN AND AROUND the church, giving his life to Jesus at age ten. He received the Holy Spirit's baptism at age twelve and started working in various areas of ministry in his early twenties. However, it wasn't until he reached his late forties that the Lord revealed to him how he had gone so many years living religiously but careless with his heart, going through the religious motions, and unwittingly accepting so many of the enemy's deceitful lies and bondages. As this new journey began, he found so many toxic counterfeit fires burning in his own life and the lives of so many Christians, and this issue was much more common in the church than most believers realized. After spending over fourteen years in law enforcement, he observed firsthand the devastating effects of sin and moral decay on families and society, living apart from the truth of Jesus Christ and the gift of His grace and love. Through this life-changing journey, Craig developed a God-given burning desire to see people everywhere transformed in the same way by recognizing the deceit and schemes of the enemy, walking in the freedom of Christ and the power of the Holy Spirit, and using that freedom to advance the kingdom of God here on earth, as it is in heaven.